Our Couple's Activity Book

A Fun and Effective Communication Workbook for Married Couples

Shana Goodwin

© **Copyright 2022 - All rights reserved.**

The content contained within this book may not be reproduced, duplicated, or transmitted without direct written permission from the author or the publisher.

Under no circumstances will any blame or legal responsibility be held against the publisher, or author, for any damages, reparation, or monetary loss due to the information contained within this book, either directly or indirectly.

Legal Notice:

This book is copyright protected. It is only for personal use. You cannot amend, distribute, sell, use, quote, or paraphrase any part, or the content within this book, without the consent of the author or publisher.

Disclaimer Notice:

Please note the information contained within this document is for educational and entertainment purposes only. All effort has been executed to present accurate, up-to-date, reliable, and complete information. No warranties of any kind are declared or implied. Readers acknowledge that the author is not engaged in rendering legal, financial, medical, or professional advice. The content within this book has been derived from various sources. Please consult a licensed professional before attempting any techniques outlined in this book.

By reading this document, the reader agrees that under no circumstances is the author responsible for any direct or indirect losses incurred as a result of the use of the information contained within this document, including, but not limited to, errors, omissions, or inaccuracies.

Contents

Introduction	v
1. Fun! Part One	1
2. Nostalgia and the Future	12
3. Date Ideas, Day or Night	30
4. He, She, They Said	42
5. Mega Millions	62
6. Fun! Part Two	72
7. Communication	81
8. 30-Day Relationship Challenge	101
9. What's Cooking, Dear?	108
Conclusion	151
Answer Sheet	155
Bibliography	161

Our Couple's Activity Book is a lighthearted activity book for married couples who want to inject some fun and love into their relationship. This book is filled with fun activities and advice from start to finish. Whether you are into word games, outdoor activities, or cooking, this book aims to cater to couples with a variety of interests to integrate dating into their daily lives. Explore fun and exciting ways to communicate with your spouse with a variety of quizzes to help you learn new things about yourself and your partner. Dating has never been this interesting!

We can only hope to achieve great things if we devote ourselves wholly and entirely to whatever we undertake. Commitment and passion are what differentiate an amazing marriage from a lackluster one.

And that's exactly the reason and purpose for this book: Easy, practical solutions to save the future existence of date night, spark communication in your relationship—and yes—have fun too! This is the 'how to' guide that will make dating, laughter, and friendship a regular activity in your relationship.

Our Couples Activity Book is a must-read for everyone interested in enhancing their marriage. Your contentment in your marriage is the cornerstone to satisfaction in all aspects of your life. Evaluate how well this special time around each other brings joy to you as a married couple and your ability to be great friends, parents, and even colleagues to others.

Throughout her dealings with others, Shana Goodwin has developed a passion for understanding communication patterns, resolving relationship differences, and understanding effective communication techniques. In *Our Couples Activity Book*, she shares with her readers what she has learned in a practical yet fun way.

Introduction

For more than a week, my friend Joanna was buzzing with excitement: The moment had finally come for her to spend some quality time with her spouse on a date. Naturally, as a wife and mother who understands the struggle, I was eager to hear how the evening went, so I called her the next day. She began the conversation by thanking me for minding the kids while they were on their date before filling me in on the details. By the tone of her voice, I could picture the complete dismay on her face. "It was a total date night disaster. We were both too tired to talk and had no idea what to do with our time alone. Dinner was nice, but there was a never-ending awkward silence. I set my expectations way too high. Shan, to be honest, the alone time without having anything to say to each other really scared me."

I don't think Joanna is the only one who has felt this way. Have you ever had the feeling that your marriage is going through a rough patch or that you're stuck in an awkward silence—like you are trapped in a connection rut? Are you and your spouse both so preoccupied with the daily hustle and bustle that when you do have some alone time, you can't think of what to do with it?

As Friedrich Nietzsche said, "It is not a lack of love, but a lack of friendship that makes unhappy marriages."

A happy marriage is not always the result of intense love. Marriage involves more than simply love, and one of those elements is indeed friendship.

Another friend of mine, Annie, had an amazing night out with her hubby, Ben. Unfortunately, they forgot all about the fun when they got home and discovered that their 5-year-old son, Andy, had locked himself in their room, leaving their eldest, Kenny—who was responsible for babysitting him—in a hysterical state because he could not get the door unlocked! Annie expressed her disappointment about the mere fact that her date night was such an effort to maintain; why couldn't it be a more natural or daily event? Annie has a point here. Why shouldn't date night be an integrated part of couples' lives rather than a once-in-a-blue-moon (and sometimes awkward) experience?

Audrey Hepburn famously said, "If I get married, I want to be very married."

We undermine ourselves when we do things roughly twice. We can only hope to achieve great things if we devote ourselves entirely and completely to whatever we undertake. Commitment and passion are what differentiate an amazing marriage from a lacklustre one.

And that's exactly the reason and purpose for this book: Easy, practical solutions to save the future existence of date night, spark communication in your relationship—and yes—have fun too! This is the 'how to' guide that will make dating, laughter, and friendship a regular activity in your relationship.

Merely sharing a living space with one's spouse may lead to a lot of irritation, tension, and even disagreement. His socks on the floor and her make-up all over the place; these seem less charming after the fifth year of marriage. It's a miracle any of us survive it through the first couple of years of marriage, considering the responsibilities of kids, money problems, and professional life, all stacked on top of the fundamental differences in how males and females look at things. Above and beyond our individual needs or difficulties, a close connection between spouses is a dynamic, ever-changing reality that should be maintained and treasured daily.

I hope that reading this book will give you the inspiration and tools you need to spend more time with your spouse, enjoy each other's company like when you first met, and improve your overall communication and marriage.

This book will teach you the essentials you need to improve your marriage through interactive games, quizzes, word searches, date night ideas, and bucket list suggestions. These activities will help you remember wonderful times you've had together, show you undiscovered things about each other, and help you make more happy memories.

My name is Shana Goodwin. I was born and raised on a farm in Arizona, where I grew up in a big family with two sisters and three brothers. My experiences as part of a large, diverse family helped me understand the differences and frustrations between couples. I grew up to become a mom with three daughters of my own. As a social worker, I deal with many different cases daily. These interactions have sparked my interest in relationship dynamics. Throughout my dealings with others, I have developed a passion for understanding communication patterns, resolving relationship differences, and understanding effective communication techniques. I greatly admire my parents' example of a long and happy marriage and find it essential to teach others the skills to improve and revitalize their relationships.

I have written this book because I care about the commitment of marriage. Just like my friends need support in their daily relationship struggles, I believe there are many other couples out there that need the same. I would like to share the experiences I have gained over the years through working with families of all kinds. Ultimately, my purpose is not only to keep families together but also, to improve their understanding of each other's roles, behaviors, and reactions.

Join me on this journey through activities, practical tips, and interactive games. I want to show you that your marriage's 'honeymoon stage' can last forever if you keep the effort real.

This book includes many different location suggestions for your time together, with some of these activities achievable at home. I recommend that you make quiet time when doing these. For instance, try them out when all your work is done; and if you have kids, when they are sleeping (for example, early morning or late night).

Our Couples Activity Book is a must-read for everyone interested in enhancing their marriage. Your contentment in your marriage is the cornerstone to satisfaction in all aspects of your life. Evaluate how well this special time around each other brings joy to you as a married couple and your ability to be great friends, parents, and even colleagues to others.

> "A successful marriage requires falling in love many times, always with the same person." – Mignon McLaughlin

Chapter 1
Fun! Part One

If you and your spouse have the same dreary routine every day, it may steal all of the sparkle from your marriage and your love of being together. Integrating simple, fun stuff for spouses is the greatest approach to shaking up the routine. This is a fun chapter with loads of simple, exciting activities like fill-in-the-blanks, word puzzles, crossword games, scrambles, and trivia to help you and your spouse break the ice.

Playing With Words

What you need to complete the activities: pen, paper, yourself, and your spouse!
Time: 5 to 15 minutes

I Love You Word Scramble

A simple and quick fun activity you can do almost anywhere. Rearrange the following words and phrases as a couple. In a loving marriage, one may say or feel the following phrases.

Next to each word or phrase, write all deciphered letters on the line. Test your ability to decode them all in a short amount of time. Answers may be found on page 155.

HTE MI ULCEIKST SNPEOR NI HET WRLOD

_____

OVLE I OUY

_____

DHLO YM HNDA

_____

OEVL OYU STOL

_____

OURY ERVEOFR NEMI

_____

SSIK EM

_____

WNNAA OG NO A TADE

_____

LVEO HET YAW UOY MESLL TNOGTHI

_____

GUH EM LPAEES

_____

ROYU ETH EBTS

_____

Add Only One Word

Engage in a word game to remind you why you fell in love with your spouse in the first place. Recalling the beautiful memories may help you not just to recollect why you chose your spouse but also renew closeness and redevelop affection for each other. Begin with any word to play *Add Only One Word*. Your spouse responds with a new word that adds to the statement. What is the aim? Describe your love tale using the words you choose as you go along. Couples, for example, can take turns uttering one word at a time to form whole phrases and create a tale. For example, you may add "We," with your spouse responding "enjoy," upon which you may say "eating," and then your spouse would answer "pizza." A similar enjoyable alphabet word game for couples would be when one person begins a word with the letter A, with the other person then creating the next word with a B, and so forth, to create the sentence (Lewine).

Love Word Search Puzzle

WORD SEARCH
Couples Love

Find the words listed in the
Word Bank

I LOVE YOU (English) • ICH LIEBE DICH (German) EK HET JOU LIEF (Afrikaans)
IK HOU VAN JOU (Dutch)
YA TEBYA LYUBLYU (Russian) SARANG HEYO (Korean) DOOSET DARAM (Farsi)
WO AI NI (Mandarin) JE TAIME (French) TI AMO (Italian) TECHIHHILA (Sioux)
TE AMO (Spanish) ANA BEHIBAK (Arabic) NGOH OI NEIH (Cantonese) IKH HOB DIKH (Yiddish)

S	C	L	M	U	O	J	N	A	V	U	O	H	K	I
A	F	D	E	G	L	I	E	B	H	I	N	E	A	K
R	G	D	O	O	S	E	T	D	A	R	A	M	B	H
A	H	N	G	O	H	O	I	N	E	I	H	I	I	H
N	I	W	O	A	I	N	I	T	E	C	H	A	H	O
G	J	H	O	B	Y	A	D	E	N	V	E	T	E	B
H	C	I	D	E	B	E	I	L	C	H	I	E	B	D
E	K	H	E	T	J	O	U	L	I	E	F	J	A	I
Y	T	E	C	H	I	H	H	I	L	A	L	A	N	K
O	M	A	I	T	T	E	A	M	O	N	O	M	A	H
Y	A	T	E	B	Y	A	L	Y	U	B	L	Y	U	G
I	L	O	V	E	Y	O	U	L	A	L	S	S	A	N

"Love and kindness are the universal
language of all creation." ~
Debasish Mridha

A word search is an activity you can do together as a couple or in competition with one another to see who finishes first. It is unique because it can be played almost anywhere without much hassle. I found a clever idea on www.education.com for a word search that describes the word "I Love You" in different languages around the world. Love is the universal factor here. This inspired me to compile the above word search for you to try. I hope you will have lots of fun with it. The answers can be found on page 155.

Multiple Choice: Couples Trivia

The Questions

Ask each other the questions below, and compare your answers to see how well you know your spouse and how well they know you.

1. What are your spouse's favorite foods?
2. Who is your partner's favorite actor or actress?
3. What is your partner's preferred outdoor activity?
4. What is the favorite book of your partner?
5. What superhero is your partner's favorite?
6. What is the favorite color of your partner?
7. Which season is your partner's favorite?
8. What sport is your partner's favorite to watch? Do you want to play it?
9. What is your partner's favorite restaurant?
10. What time of day does your partner prefer, and why? (Schwanke)

Quiz on Couples Communication

1. What is my preferred method of showing love? Gifts? Touch? Random acts of kindness? Spending time together?
2. What is my preferred method of getting affection?
3. What type of person do you think I am: An introvert or an extrovert?
4. What do I mean when I say "argument"?
5. What do I enjoy discussing at the end of each day?
6. Is it possible for me to quickly recognize my emotions?

Fill in the Missing Words

Attempt a "fill in the missing word" activity. This could be fun if one partner knows the answers and the other needs to guess. It also helps you to learn to know each other's thoughts. Decide ahead of time regarding who will be the one to write the story. Don't show your partner the story until they have completed all the open spaces! In the sequence specified under each blank line, that individual will yell out each word prompt. Allow your spouse to say whatever comes to mind and write it down in the blank area provided. At the end of them completing the letter, read it aloud.

"Dear _____ (spouse's name)

My favorite memory of us is when we _____. The best time we ever spent together was when _____ .

On our first date, we met at _____ and our first drinks together were _____. I wore a _____ and you wore _____. The thing about you I like the most is _____.

Love from,

_____"

Fill the following in about yourself, and about each other:

My special talent is _____

My childhood nickname is _____

My favorite holiday is _____

My favorite movie is _____

My childhood dream job was _____

My favorite ice cream flavor is _____

I love to eat _____

My best friend is _____

I hate it when someone _____

My best moment so far was when _____

Read the answers to one another and count how many answers you got right. The winner may choose something the other spouse needs to do for an entire week for them as a prize.

Couples Crossword Fun

The fancies of love and passion are the focus of this easy crossword problem. Set a timer to see how quickly you can do it as a team. Find the answers on page 155.

ACROSS
3 He snores
4 Amount of money after paying bills
5 Don't go to bed _____
6 Best feeling in the World
9 Effective relationship skill
10 Let it Go

DOWN
1 Favorite working day
2 Couples need this
3 Holiday after getting married
7 Happy Valentines __!
8 She smells really good

Try to do more couple's crosswords and better your time.

Have some more fun by creating your own personalized couple crossword puzzle. An example of a crossword creator is https://www.puzzle-maker.com/.

Multimedia Couple's Artwork

What you will need:

- Sheeting
- Cuts of cloth
- Whatever else you may desire for a multimedia project (it's entirely your choice!)
- Canvas or paper for your creation
- Pens
- Paint, brushes
- Glue
- Old pictures and newspapers
- Pencils
- Markers
- Scissors
- Blindfolds

Timeline: 1 to 1 ½ hours

How do you actually view one another? Utilize what you have available at home to make a multimedia work of art of each other while being blindfolded. You can select a mix of ink, paint, colored pencils, fabric, paper, beads, and other art tools available. This one will likely generate some chuckles, including during the exercise and afterward.

Steps:

1. Initially, organize the workspaces: Lay the sheeting down, organize all your acquired objects within range, and establish the canvases or paper for your masterpieces. If you wish to utilize clippings from newspapers or magazines, then cut some out.

2. Put on eye masks. Use what is available to make pictures of one another while your eyes are still covered.
3. Inspect your paintings and have a nice giggle after the blindfolds are removed. Hint: Choose whether you want to try your luck with both of you being blinded at the same moment. If not, you may take turns assisting each other while refraining from making much more of a mess. You can also choose to eliminate the face masks entirely if you like (Schwanke).

Lovers' Tic-tac-Toe

Guidelines to Play

This modified game of Tic-Tac-Toe aims to acquire three points in a row on the board. The game is played on a 3-by 3-grid game square.

The very first player is referred to as ♥, while the second player is referred to as O.

When one opponent has three in a row, or until all nine spaces on the game board have been filled, the players alternate putting ♥ s and Os on the playing area.

♥ is always the first to go; if no one manages to get three in a row, the match is referred to as a tie (Holme).

"Happily ever after" is not a fairy tale. It's a choice.

— Fawn Weaver

Chapter 2
Nostalgia and the Future

We can become so involved in the present moment and all its needs and problems that we often forget to look back on the wonderful times we have shared together and the memories made as a couple. When a loved one passes away, we compile a collection of photographs and reflect on the happy times shared. But why wait? We must celebrate each other and our good memories while we are still here.

Nostalgia

One of the nicest things you can say to your wife or husband is, "If I had to do it over again, I'd choose you again" (Unknown).

Write Your Unique Love Story

If you've been in a marriage for a lengthy period, you may have stretches of time where you believe you've outgrown your passion for your spouse. This is called "love fatigue." Perhaps you've changed as individuals during your relationship, or maybe you're amid another stage of your relationship with your spouse, which is why you're starting to feel uneasy. When a couple is in love, their experiences together might be substantially distorted, either during the marriage or after it has ended. When people are in love, their brains are intrinsically stronger at producing memories. Can those moments remain in perpetuity without being tarnished? No. Love feelings are very fragile. Take a good look at some other couples; you will see a range of cases where there are disagreements (apparent contradictions) between how they recall an event and how their spouse remembers it. Because of the complex feelings created during personal love, biases will infiltrate the recognition memory associated with love in various ways.

The Most Serious Points

Boring interactions are an indication that something is wrong between two people. But what if there's really nothing broken with the situation, and this is merely a snag in the relationship's regular progression? Lovers often express such sentiments as "feeling hollow in our marriage" or "There's no fire in our connection." We know you may have had hatred for each other at one point, but perhaps there was a shift in something later in the process. Alternatively, you may have developed a relationship with your spouse at an initial glance, astonished that someone could relate to you so perfectly. Each of you may have come from difficult backgrounds, and thus, you may be surprised to find yourselves in such good hands. All of these tales tell us more about the origins of a connection and illustrate the attractiveness of closeness in its purest form. Every pleasant memory will initiate closeness in some way or another. Restoring closeness will demolish any concrete barriers that may exist between you and your relationship. Even if you just take down one stone, you are creating more room for love to enter.

Furthermore, reminiscing will provide clues as to how much power or energy you can generate from this connection. Consequently, remembering will provide you with a sense of optimism and motivation. Bear in mind that you have already fulfilled your relationship, and this will assist you in staying on the right track. It's all too easy to lose track of how tirelessly you've fought to begin creating your connection in the first place. It may appear that it occurred by magical enchantment, but this was not the case; you were the one who conjured up the dream. You built a particular relationship between you and your partner by paying close attention to one another, with the emphasis placed on demonstrating your affection. The following themes might be used to start a couple's story-telling session. You may make a list of responses to the questions by discussing them with your spouse. Complete this activity as a group, or use it as a starting point for a dialogue with others. It is possible that your spouse will not wish to participate in this experiment with you, but you may still consider it to be a useful tool.

1. When and how did you first meet?
2. What were your initial impressions of your spouse when you first met them?
3. When you first started dating them, what was it that attracted you to them?
4. What was it that first attracted you to them?
5. When did you realize you were head over heels in love with your companion?
6. When you went on your first date, what exactly did you do?

7. What did you like the most about your first date and why?
8. When or how did you first notice that this connection differed from others?
9. What prompted you to believe or feel that this connection will be unique in any way?
10. What were your spouse's thoughts about this new connection, exactly?
11. What was your family's response to this news?
12. Have you ever had to overcome any obstacles in your relationship?
13. What were your thoughts on the manner in which you communicated?
14. What activities have you and your partner enjoyed doing together?
15. Over the years, how much have you and your partner nurtured each other?
16. What is your fondest recollection of the time you two spent together?

Prepare your responses in advance. In a gentle approach, the questions posed above might assist you in remembering your unique love tale from the past. You should also consider answering such queries if you wish to improve the angle of your connection. As an awakening thread in your love story reconstruction, copy the responses consecutively into the provided area below, or write them down on paper (Holme).

Spouse A: Answers

1. _____
2. _____
3. _____
4. _____
5. _____
6. _____
7. _____
8. _____
9. _____
10. _____
11. _____
12. _____
13. _____
14. _____
15. _____
16. _____
17. _____
18. _____
19. _____
20. _____

Spouse B: Answers

1. _____
2. _____
3. _____
4. _____
5. _____
6. _____
7. _____
8. _____
9. _____
10. _____
11. _____
12. _____
13. _____
14. _____
15. _____
16. _____
17. _____
18. _____
19. _____
20. _____

Playing Couple's Tag

Questionnaire: First Day

1. When and where did we meet for the first time?

   ----

2. Where did we go on our first date?

   ----

3. What was your initial reaction to me?

   ----

4. When did you first meet my relatives?

   ----

5. Who was the first to say "I love you"?

   ----

6. What is my favorite piece of clothing?

   ----

7. Is it possible that we have a strange behavior in common?

_____

_____

8. What do I usually do in my spare time?

_____

_____

9. What is my favorite thing about you?

_____

_____

Questionnaire: Second Day

Is it true that we've been together for a long time?

_____

_____

2. When was the first time we went on a road trip?

_____

_____

3. What was the first thing that you noticed about me?

_____

_____

4. What are the most common points of conflict between us?

_____

_____

5. Do I have any strange habits?

_____

_____

6. What are our nicknames for each other?

_____

_____

7. What irritates you the most about me?

_____

_____

8. What am I not very good at?

_____

_____

9. What is your favorite thing about me?

_____

_____

Creating a Time Capsule Box

"A happy marriage is about three things: Memories of togetherness, the forgiveness of mistakes, and a promise to never give up on each other." -Surabhi Surendra

Take a lockable box and identify some of your favorite memories like love letters, unique tokens of affection, etcetera. Put them in the box and bury it in a safe place. Agree on a date to open it together and reminisce about your special moments.

The Future

"Happy marriages look for the future, not the past." -Dale Partridge

While reflecting on the past and celebrating happy moments, discussing the future, your individual and joint goals, and how you would like to achieve them is important. With the blessing of marriage, you get the distinct privilege of looking forward with eager expectations for the future. This sometimes involves developing day-to-day plans, and sometimes it entails preparing something genuinely spectacular for two years into the future.

Take some time to complete the following tasks:

- Make a plan ahead of time
- Discuss your objectives
- Prepare for the future as a team

Whenever you share your thoughts with someone, a variety of situations necessitate planning ahead of time. You'll need to plan exciting activities for the whole family, design a budget, anticipate potential issues, and pick where you'll spend your holiday. Commit yourself to allocating time every month to arrange these activities.

Take the time to think about and prepare for your main ambitions, such as taking a particular vacation or purchasing a car or home. Working with others to achieve a common objective may be incredibly rewarding and gratifying.

You and your spouse have goals for your family, your personal life, and your finances that you should share with one another. It is good to talk over your goals occasionally throughout the year to ensure that you are taking steps now to assist you in achieving your objectives. Talking about your dreams with a partner might allow you to define them better.

The future holds a plethora of opportunities for you and your spouse, from commemorating your anniversary to just having a lovely time during the relaxation of your retirement. In addition to enjoying your children's successes, you may look forward to reaping the benefits of their efforts. Discuss the events and experiences you are most excited about with your spouse and how you plan to spend your time. Keep in mind that half of the enjoyment is in the suspense!

Your marriage has the ability to be one of the most rewarding experiences of your life. Just continue to speak with your spouse on a regular basis, be genuine partners in living, make sure to invest time and effort into your marriage, be adaptable, and give your marriage your complete and total devotion.

Most spouses devote weeks or even months of their time and effort to planning the "ideal" wedding. Every element is studied, and a decision is reached. Strategies for contingencies are developed, timelines are completed, and preparations are meticulously managed and structured ahead of time. There is even a practice run for the festivities on the big day. No element is left to chance; each conceivable scenario is accounted for and taken into consideration.

Nevertheless, how many couples devote even a portion of their time to wedding day preparations to marriage preparedness? How many people make any preparations for their marriage? The day after they say "I Do," they awaken as a married couple, and they will live together with each other for the coming years while they negotiate their path to "happily ever after." Unfortunately, nearly one-half of all marriages end up in divorce, which means that many will never get to their happily ever after.

Incorporate the following attributes into your daily life: Love, peace, joy, patience, kindness, goodness, gentleness, and self-control. You will be strong on your way to designing an effective plan for a happy marriage. Examine this one by one, and explore how you and your spouse can put them to use to strengthen your marriage. Take a look at your own life and consider how you may utilize them to better your marriage and other personal relationships.

Activity: What Has Marriage Taught You?

I have learned some things from my parents, family, friends, and especially my own marriage:

- Life is fleeting, and love is a wilting flower
- If you desire anything, you must first give it to someone else
- Make a difference by being the change you wish to see in the world
- Life continues whether or not we are actively involved in it

- If you are in a dark place, the safest route out is to pursue the sound of your own voice, stating that the light and the truth are love
- My motivation for existence has absolutely nothing to do with me
- Just because life gets crazy, that doesn't mean I have to be
- Love is the foundation upon which reconciliation is built

Each partner must make a list of ten things that marriage has taught them. Then, adding to the list, they need to state how they will use this knowledge in the future.

Spouse A:

1. _____
2. _____
3. _____
4. _____
5. _____
6. _____
7. _____
8. _____
9. _____
10. _____

Spouse B:

1. _____
2. _____
3. _____
4. _____
5. _____
6. _____
7. _____
8. _____
9. _____
10. _____

Envision the Future Word Search

Envisioning the Future

```
U  A  F  F  E  C  T  I  O  N  F  D  E  A
M  I  I  Y  P  P  A  H  I  C  E  D  L  P
O  I  C  O  N  N  E  C  T  E  D  M  E  P
S  P  M  N  U  X  R  E  H  T  E  G  O  T
U  C  O  M  M  U  N  I  C  A  T  I  O  N
P  P  T  M  S  O  D  L  O  T  I  M  E  N
P  S  M  P  N  P  E  O  M  N  E  I  I  S
O  I  E  D  M  S  D  V  M  L  E  D  D  E
R  H  E  X  N  R  E  E  I  U  E  U  D  D
T  T  N  I  C  I  V  D  T  F  I  T  P  A
I  D  F  M  U  E  O  C  T  Y  O  F  O  N
V  T  S  T  T  E  T  O  E  A  M  D  E  C
E  O  Y  A  E  T  E  Y  D  L  D  C  D  N
V  M  O  C  G  T  D  O  D  P  I  G  E  H
```

TOGETHER
HAPPY
SEX
AFFECTION
PLAYFUL
COMMUNICATION
LOVED
DEVOTED
CONNECTED
TIME
SUPPORTIVE
COMMITTED

Play this puzzle online at : https://thewordsearch.com/puzzle/3481274/

Download the word search on Envisioning the Future at thewordsearch.com.

View the answers on page 155.

Questionnaire: First Day

1. Do you have a personal objective you want to accomplish over the next five years?

_____

_____

2. Was there something you've always wanted to know about me that you'd like to know?

_____

_____

3. What's the one thing you'd alter right now, and why?

_____

_____

4. Which country do you want us to visit that you haven't been to yet?

_____

_____

5. What do you hope to accomplish in your lifetime?

_____

_____

> "We come to love not by finding a perfect person, but by learning to see an imperfect person perfectly."
>
> — Sam Keen, *To Love and Be Loved*

Questionnaire: Second Day

1. Are you more afraid of being abandoned or being smothered with affection?

_____

_____

2. Do you like to keep talking until you find a solution in the thick of the fight? Or do you break away, think about it, and come back to it at a later time? Which is more effective?

_____

_____

3. What would you do if I had a disagreement with a member of your family?

_____

_____

4. What would you do with $5,000 if we won it?

_____

_____

5. How much time alone do you require?

_____

_____

Chapter 3
Date Ideas, Day or Night

Many married couples battle to define what it means to go on a "date night," as the phrase goes. A date night is a scheduled evening when a devoted pair takes time away from their kids and other commitments to spend time together. These can be date days too, but the important thing is that the couple spends time together. Date night entails a sensation of escaping the mundane everyday life. You put on a different outfit, go to a different location, or participate in an unusual activity. Married couples' dates should be one-of-a-kind.

I am sure you're aware that dates are essential for healthy marriages. Even so, you probably don't have one too often (it may be especially difficult to schedule date days if you have children or a busy job.)

You're undoubtedly also aware of the obvious reasons why dates are important: They promote communication, boost feelings of closeness, reduce the likelihood of taking each other for granted, reduce stress, and nurture connection.

You're not alone in not prioritizing date night, as important as each of these obvious reasons may be. Why? Because we're often too busy to add anything more to our packed calendars. We may also take our lover or relationship for granted because we place a high value on our children and working responsibilities.

If you and your spouse haven't yet adopted spending regular, concentrated quality time around each other, here are a few reasons why dates are something you should really explore:

Dates help couples stay connected through intimate communication, care, and support. This also reduces the stress in their minds and in their relationships. We don't always have to make the right connections with our spouses; nonetheless, we must maintain and grow our ability to pay attention and be totally present to our spouses when they are anxious, as well as our ability to be steadfastly devoted and dependable friend. A mix of activities that appeal to both spouses and emphasize new and different experiences can help to boost connection.

Check out each date idea on the list below, and soon enough, you'll be changing up your usual dining and movie date routine. From this list, try anything that is really new and unique (Schumer):

Bring Back the Fun to Date Night

Do a Picnic

When the weather is beautiful, there's nothing more romantic than packing up some cozy drinks and snacks, laying out a blanket, and enjoying the outdoors. If the weather is bad out, simply relocate the gathering indoors.

Go Hiking

After that, go for a hike to get some fresh air. Prepare a picnic basket or a snack, and spend some time relaxing at the top of the mountain, soaking all this in. It is also a perfect moment to take some spectacular photos.

Take a Road Trip to a New Place

Allow yourself to be a free spirit and discover where the path leads you! Make a game board with different numbered locations. Take turns rolling dice before each trip, and watch where you land.

Do an Escape Room Game

An Escape Room Game is a fantastic option for a double date with your best friends, with venues growing in many cities across the country. You will learn a lot about your spouse. Nothing brings out the "true you," like the pressure of having to complete the task in a specific amount of time.

Paint Pottery Together at a Clay Cafe or Class

Even if neither of you are artists, taking a pottery class allows you to learn new skills. Don't take yourself too seriously; remember, it's okay to laugh at yourself. At the end of your date, you'll have something to take home as a special memory.

Go Camping as a Couple

Camping is an outdoor activity you either really enjoy or absolutely despise; you will need to try it to know. Before you leave, talk it over with each other and resolve that if one of you doesn't like it at any moment, you'll pack up your belongings and find a room to stay in for the rest of the time.

Have a Couples Game Night

Couples may have a lot of fun playing party games together. Invite another couple to bring over their favorite foods and drinks, and you're sure to have a great time together. Consider one of the entertaining double date game night activities!

Playing Charades! on Your Phone

Depending on the category you pick, Charades! will have you dancing, singing, and acting out hints. The app is free (at the time of writing this book) and has over 100 kinds of activities to play. Divide into groups, couple versus couple, or men versus women, and see who wins.

If the Shoe Fits, Wear It

This is a fun game to see how well you and your spouse really know one another. You take off your shoes, give one to your spouse and take one from your spouse, creating physical symbols for every individual. Then you sit back-to-back so neither of you can see another or your responses. Someone will start by asking you questions, such as, "Who is more likely to win?" Then, you raise the shoe of the individual to whom you believe the statement or question applies.

Do a Paint Night Together

Classes in painting with wine and snacks on the side are becoming more widely popular. Find one near you and bring your spouse. If you'd prefer to have your date at home, pick up some paint, a couple of canvas and brushes, and follow an online lesson.

Go Out Dancing

This doesn't necessarily have to be at a nightclub. You might even go to a nice pub and try your hand at true country-style line dancing!

Make It a Dessert Date

I scream for a great date night, you scream for a great date night, we all scream for delicious ice cream! Create an ice cream bar with different toppings and sauces to choose from. Enjoy your ice cream over a nice chat.

Learn to Speak a New Language

We understand that you won't be able to become completely proficient in one night. However, learning a new language collaboratively is a fun and informative continuous undertaking, and it also means you have a teammate. In the new language, tell each other that you adore each other.

Create a Scrapbook Together

Many of us don't have a lot of photos in physical form in this age of mobile photography. Print out some of your absolute favorites, buy a scrapbooking package, and design and keep your memories safe for generations to come.

Make a Cocktail Date

Learn how to mix your favorite drinks at home instead of crowding together into a busy bar and yelling over the other people. Not only will mixing them yourself save you money, but it will also teach you a fresh talent that you can flaunt at a future social event.

Find a Spot to Watch the Sunset Together

Find the most gorgeous spot you can, bring some coffee, and sit and enjoy the sunset—or even the sunrise. Simply relax and allow the magnificence of the sky to touch your heart with peace and joy.

Play Video Games Together

Try playing games together on your favorite console or a phone or tablet. Enjoy competing against each other or helping one another solve a puzzle or challenging quiz.

Bucket List Brainstorming for Couples

In *The Bucket List Activity Book for Couples*, Dr. Carol Morgan lists excellent ideas for exploring each other's interests and determining what should be on your own unique couple's bucket list. Some activities are explored below, and you are welcome also to add some of your own.

Dream About Winning the Lottery Game

Imagine you won the lottery. For example, say you won more than $1 million to share as a couple. What are your expectations, and how will you be spending it?

Spouse A:

Spouse B:

Which of the above will still be priorities for you to reach, even if you do not win the lottery? Are there any other ways of achieving these objectives, and how?

The Couples Guessing Game

"I have never, ever in my life done the following..." This game will help you get to know each other and what you have not done before. Once you have completed your lists of "nevers," discuss these and determine why you have never done them before. Is it because you are afraid? Because you never had the opportunity, are they something you would like to do? Or, perhaps, are they something you have not done because you really have no interest in doing them?

Spouse A - I Have Never, Ever:

1. _____
2. _____
3. _____
4. _____
5. _____
6. _____
7. _____
8. _____
9. _____
10. _____

Spouse B - I Have Never, Ever:

1. _____
2. _____
3. _____
4. _____
5. _____
6. _____
7. _____
8. _____
9. _____
10. _____

Discovering a New Recipe or Meal

Decide on a new recipe together. You can create your own or search online for an unknown recipe that you would like to try. After planning the recipe, gathering the ingredients, and preparing it, you can sit down as a couple and enjoy the meal. Talk about ideas for further recipes, restaurants, and even different cultures' cooking that you would like to explore in the future.

Around the World Online

Watch YouTube videos of different countries and travel destinations. Discuss with one another which places you would like to visit and why.

Spouse A: Dream Destinations

1. _____
2. _____
3. _____

Spouse B: Dream Destinations

1. _____
2. _____
3. _____

Create a Vision Board Collage

Use the internet and magazines to search for pictures that relate to your objectives. Print, cut out, and paste or stick these to cardboard, corkboard, or any other type of board that you can place in a prominent spot in your home. The vision board should be a combination of both partners' future goals and dreams. It may include various aspects such as your home, finances, dream jobs, dream cars, goals for your kids, or a place you would like to relocate to, for example.

Now, list these objectives below, accompanied by possible steps you can take to get closer to achieving these goals:

Spouse A:

1. _____
2. _____
3. _____
4. _____
5. _____
6. _____
7. _____
8. _____
9. _____
10. _____

Spouse B:

1. _____
2. _____
3. _____
4. _____
5. _____
6. _____
7. _____
8. _____
9. _____
10. _____

Your Couple's Bucket List

The following is your Personal Couple's Bucket List:

Spouse A:

1. _____
2. _____
3. _____
4. _____
5. _____
6. _____
7. _____

Spouse B:

1. _____
2. _____
3. _____
4. _____
5. _____
6. _____
7. _____

Chapter 4
He, She, They Said

"Diversity: the art of thinking independently together."

— Malcolm Forbes

Jokes regarding people's differences are ageless and practically endless in kind. They're recounted at celebrations, discussed over drinks, and viewed and sent to friends and coworkers as texts. We chuckle at these funny anecdotes, but is it truly the case? Is it true that individuals are so significantly different?

The questions below may also be used for the Shoe Game explained in Chapter 3. Although this may be a popular game at wedding receptions, it is also a great game to play when already married for a while. It's a great way to learn about yourself and your spouse and share some laughter while doing it.

He, She, They Said Questions

Guess Who the Statement Is About

1. I am the first who said: "I love you."
2. I proposed.
3. I first met my future in-laws.
4. I initiated the first kiss.
5. I am a prankster.
6. I am the most inventive.
7. I am the best cook.
8. I am always right.
9. I wear the pants in our relationship.
10. I am most likely to be late.
11. I am the most prone to getting lost.
12. I am the most amusing.
13. I am the patient one.
14. I'm the one taking responsibility for the spider in the house.
15. I'm the cranky one in the morning.
16. I'm the clumsy one.
17. I'm the more capable driver.
18. At a wedding, I'll be the first one to cry.
19. I am the more skilled dancer.
20. I'm the one who takes the most selfies.
21. I steal the covers while sleeping.
22. I'm the one who makes people laugh.
23. When I'm driving, I'm the one who is most likely to get lost.
24. I take very long showers.
25. When I'm sick, I'm the biggest baby.
26. I fart the most.

27. I'm the one who is most inclined to buy anything impulsively.
28. I devote the most time to wedding preparations.
29. I'm the one who snores the most.
30. I'm far more persistent.
31. I'm better at folding clothes.
32. I occupy most of the mattress.
33. I have the most pairs of sneakers.
34. I'm the boss of the remote control.
35. I'm much more romantic.
36. My pals are the most irritating.
37. When I'm driving, I'm the most likely to run out of gas.
38. I paid for the first date.
39. I organized the honeymoon.
40. I was the first one to update my Facebook relationship status.
41. I'm the one that wants the most children.
42. I'm the best bargain hunter.
43. I usually come out on top in fights.
44. In our relationship, I'm the grumpy one.
45. I have the most traffic tickets.
46. I have the biggest feet.
47. I have the poorest eyesight.
48. I have the most terrible hearing.
49. My family is the craziest!

She, He, They Want Questions

Answer whichever set of questions applies to you (or both sets, if applicable):

Set A - Questions

Go over the statements below. Mark the ones that, if spoken by your spouse, would cause you to feel far more cherished.

- "You look tired. Allow me to give you a back rub."
- "Thank you for all you do for us. I bought you a special gift."
- "It seems like you had a hard day. Do you want to talk about it? What happened?"
- "I absolutely love your new hairstyle." It brings out your beautiful eyes."
- "Those packages look quite big." Allow me to carry them for you."
- "I have a few people in my office, but I'd like to know what's bothering you. Hold on for a moment, and I'll take your call in a private area where we may chat without distractions" (In reaction to your phone call to him at the office, seeming angry and requesting to speak to him).

Go over the statements below. Mark the ones that, if spoken by your spouse, would cause you to feel less cherished.

- "I'm in the middle of watching a baseball game. Can't you see that? You always want to chat when I'm trying to watch my sports."

- "I know tomorrow is your birthday, but I've been swamped. Please, take my credit card and spend $100 on yourself."
- "I hear Jack's wife went to a new gym class and lost 12 pounds. Perhaps you would like to go and try it out—it may help you feel better about your weight?"
- "When are you planning to clean our house? It's really messy."
- "Will you please scratch my back? I need some attention from my wife."

Set B - Questions

Go over the statements below. Mark the ones that, if spoken by your spouse, would cause you to feel far more valued.

- "The garage door doesn't want to open, and I know you're better at mechanical things. Will you have a look, please?"
- "My husband took the kids to the zoo yesterday to give me some off-time. He's really making an effort to give me some rest when I need it."
- "I'm so proud of you for getting a promotion at work. You deserve it after all your hard work."
- "I'm experiencing a difficult time at the office with my co-worker - he has been discussing me with my boss. What will you suggest I do about it?"
- "Thank you for the gift. It really made my day, and I totally love it!"

Go over the statements below. Mark the ones that, if spoken by your spouse, would cause you to feel less cherished.

- "You're not that good at fixing stuff—why not phone a pro to repair it?" "Stop acting irresponsibly; when will you stop spending so much time on your dream of starting a business?"
- "Technical skills are not really my husband's strength." "Yesterday, it took him five hours to figure out how to set up our new PC."
- "We need more income to get these bills paid. I am already doing an extra job after hours. When are you going to start making more money at your job or get a side hustle?
- "I didn't get you that smartwatch for your birthday; it was just too expensive. I thought new clothes would be more responsible."

Vacation and Other Questionnaires

This category contains a plethora of questions since most people have a strong interest in travel. It's a treat to spend some time kicking back, exploring, or soaking up the world's culture with someone who shares a passion for travel. All couple's vacations, in my opinion, are relationship retreats, an occasion for enjoyment that brings spouses closer together.

- Do you enjoy experiencing different ways of life, or do you find it frustrating that other countries or areas don't do things as efficiently or as well as you do back home?
- Have you ever traveled outside of the country? Do you have a passport? When does it expire?
- Do you usually conduct some business while on vacation (email, voicemail, phone calls, etcetera)?

- How much time do you spend per day? Is that really necessary?
- Would you rather take a $6000 vacation for a week a year, a $3000 vacation twice a year, or would you rather spend $2000 on three separate one-week breakaways?
- What is the longest vacation you think you could take according to your schedule without causing a problem at work or with your income?
- Where would you take your spouse if you could plan any vacation?
- What is your usual goal when traveling (relax, sightsee, have new experiences, visit family)?
- Do you return to the same places over and over again, or do you visit new places most of the time when you travel?
- Do you like spur-of-the-moment adventures?
- How often do you travel? What are some past business and personal trips you have taken?

Individual Quizzes for Couples

For example, even if you've been married for 30 years, it's possible that you don't remember the specific Halloween treat your spouse loved the most as a child, the approximate amount of selfies they snap each week, or an alternative name that your partner might have wished they had been given when they were born. But don't be concerned; you'll have learned everything you needed to know more at these questions' conclusion. The reality that you are distinct persons with your own ideas, goals, and struggles that your spouse may be unaware of does not matter, whether you have been together for decades or have just been together for a short period of time.

These tests will provide you with several opportunities to learn a great deal more about one another. Each quiz occurs twice in the section below. Spouse A first reads and responds on their copy of the quiz, after which they hand the book to Spouse B, who then reads and responds on their copy of the quiz. Once you've finished the assignment, you may read over each other's answers, take in what you've learned, and add your scores for that chapter together. Unless otherwise stated, every quiz question is awarded one credit, unless otherwise stated.

Quiz 1: Your Spouse's Favorite Things

Spouse A

1. Describe your partner's favorite type of pillow:

    a. Memory foam

    b. Down

    c. Polyester

    d. Buckwheat

    e. Microbead

    f. Contour

    g. Body pillow

2. Your partner's favorite freebies are:

    a. Free phone applications

    b. Food samples

    c. Airline eye masks

d. Guesthouse toiletries

e. Other: _____

3. Your companion would like a non-alcoholic/alcoholic drink to assist them in relaxing (highlight one).

4. Your partner's favorite reading material belongs to the category of:

　　a. Fiction

　　b. Autobiographies

　　c. Self-help books

　　d. Internet / social media news

　　e. Other: _____

5. (True/False) Your companion likes to wear raunchy underwear.

6. Your spouse's favorite Halloween candy as a youngster was:

　　a. Cotton candy

　　b. Licorice

　　c. Smarties

　　d. M&M's

　　e. Milk chocolate

　　f. Other: _____

7. List any "favorite thing" with personal significance your partner likes wearing:

_____

8. Your spouse's most efficient time of day is:

    a. Morning (5 to 11 a.m.)

    b. Afternoon (12 to 5 p.m.)

    c. Night (6 to 10 p.m.)

    d. Late night (11 p.m. to 4 a.m.)

9. (True/False) Your spouse picks toilet paper rolls focusing on lifespan above smoothness.

10. Your partner's preferred manner to connect is:

    a. Text

    b. E-mail

    c. Face-to-face

    d. Phone

    e. Video call/FaceTime

    f. Handwritten notes or letters (Muñozz)

Spouse A Total: _____

Spouse B

1. Describe your partner's favorite type of pillow:

   a. Memory foam

   b. Down

   c. Polyester

   d. Buckwheat

   e. Microbead

   f. Contour

   g. Body pillow

2. Your partner's favorite freebies are:

   a. Free phone applications

   b. Food samples

   c. Airline eye masks

   d. Guesthouse toiletries

   e. Other: _____

3. Your companion would like a non-alcoholic / alcoholic drink to assist them in relaxing (highlight one).

4. Your partner's favorite reading material belongs to the category of:

   a. Fiction

   b. Autobiographies

c. Self-help books

d. Internet / social media news

e. Other: _____

5. (True/False) Your companion likes to wear raunchy underwear.

6. Your spouse's favorite Halloween candy as a youngster was:

    a. Cotton candy

    b. Licorice

    c. Smarties

    d. M&M's

    e. Milk chocolate

    f. Other: _____

7. List any "favorite thing" with personal significance your partner likes wearing:

_____

8. Your spouse's most efficient time of day is:

    a. Morning (5 to 11 a.m.)

    b. Afternoon (12 to 5 p.m.)

    c. Night (6 to 10 p.m.)

    d. Late night (11 p.m. to 4 a.m.)

9. (True/False) Your spouse picks toilet paper rolls focusing on lifespan above smoothness.

10. Your partner's preferred manner to connect is:

    a. Texting

    b. E-mail

    c. Face-to-face

    d. Phone

    e. Video call/FaceTime

    f. Handwritten notes or letters (Muñoz)

Spouse B Total: _____

Quiz 2: Bigger Things

This quiz is based on a questionnaire composed initially by Muñoz in *The Couple's Quiz Book: 350 Fun Questions to Energize Your Relationship*. This book is a wonderful option if you would like to communicate with your spouse through more fun quizzes.

Spouse A

1. If your spouse bought a villa, they'd spend most of their time in the:

    a. State-of-the-art kitchen

    b. Multilevel luxury garage

    c. Swimming pool

    d. Greenhouse

    e. Other: _____

2. If your spouse was picked to create a new, nationally broadcast, professional athletic event, it would most likely entail the following:

_____

3. Your partner's favorite section of the country is the:

    a. Northeast

    b. Midwest

    c. South

    d. West

    e. Other: _____

4. (True/False) Your partner plans to work after retirement.

5. The thought guru or expert whose opinions your partner presently most admires is :

_____

6. Your partner's favorite holiday destination is:

    a. On a beach

    b. On a boat/cruise ship

    c. In the mountains

    d. At home, lazing on the sofa

    e. At a wildlife reserve or animal sanctuary

    f. In a large city

    g. In an exotic rainforest

7. Highlight the phrases that best represent the construction style your spouse favors:

Modern, floor-to-ceiling windows, multiple floors, historic look, ranch, colonial, mid-century, contemporary, victorian, minimalist, American, craftsman, brownstone, farmhouse, Italian.

8. Your partner's favorite job would be best defined as:

    a. Their current job

    b. Service-related

    c. High-risk/high-excitement

    d. Creative

    e. Technology-related

    f. Advocacy work

9. The pattern your spouse feels most drawn to is:

    a. Tartan

    b. Contrast

    c. Argyle

    d. Houndstooth

    e. Rhinestone

    f. Paisley

    g. Polka dots

    h. Stripes

10. (Highlight one) Would your partner rather achieve riches quickly (e.g., lottery, scheme, inheritance) or via hard work?

SPOUSE A TOTAL: ____

Spouse B

1. If your spouse bought a villa, they'd spend most of their time in the:

    a. State-of-the-art kitchen

    b. Multilevel luxury garage

    c. Swimming pool

    d. Greenhouse

    e. Other: _____

2. If your spouse was picked to create a new, nationally broadcast, professional athletic event, it would most likely entail the following:

_____

3. Your partner's favorite section of the country is the:

    a. Northeast

    b. Midwest

    c. South

    d. West

    e. Other: _____

4. (True/False) Your partner plans to work after retirement.

5. The thought guru or expert whose opinions your partner presently most admires is

----

6. Your partner's favorite holiday destination is:

    a. On a beach

    b. On a boat/cruise ship

    c. In the mountains

    d. At home, lazing on the sofa

    e. At a wildlife reserve or animal sanctuary

    f. In a large city

    g. In an exotic rainforest

7. Highlight the three phrases that best represent the construction style your spouse favors:

Modern, floor-to-ceiling windows, multiple floors, historic look, ranch, colonial, mid-century, contemporary, victorian, minimalist, American, craftsman, brownstone, farmhouse, Italian.

8. Your partner's favorite job would be best defined as:

    a. Their current job

    b. Service-related

    c. High risk/high excitement

    d. Creative

    e. Technology-related

f. Advocacy work

9. The pattern your spouse feels most drawn to is:

   a. Tartan

   b. Contrast

   c. Argyle

   d. Houndstooth

   e. Rhinestone

   f. Paisley

   g. Polka dots

   h. Stripes

10. (Highlight one) Would your partner rather achieve riches quickly (e.g., lottery, scheme, inheritance) or via hard work?

SPOUSE B TOTAL: ____

Love Language Quiz

Visit the following link: https://www.5lovelanguages.com/quizzes/love-language and determine your Love Language™ (Chapman). This quiz will help you discover your primary love language, what this means, and how you can use it to your advantage to initiate more successful connections with your spouse and others. You need to print, share, or save your results for future use as soon as you are done because the site does not save them automatically.

Intimacy Quiz

Physical intimacy is very important in a relationship. People who don't get along in bed end up breaking up at some point or another. People anticipate that their partners will keep them satisfied in bed, but it can be hard to keep things running smoothly in the bedroom. Couples who become parents, have different sexual needs, get sick and can't have sex, or work away from home often may affect their intimate lives.

1. How does your sex life make you feel?

    - I feel happy when I think about my sex life
    - My partner and I both enjoy our sex lives
    - I'm worried that I'm not having as much fun as I should be
    - It's good enough; I just don't have a chance to think about it often

2. What does sex mean to you?

    - The intimacy and connectedness I have with my partner
    - A way to have a good relationship with someone
    - Satisfaction and pleasure
    - It's something we don't have very often

3. Do you think your sex life could get better?

    - Anything is plausible, but I'm happy already
    - Yes, a little
    - No, not at all
    - Do I have to answer at all?

4. How does your spouse handle intimacy?

- They are very interested in it
- Most of the time, they are happy to do it
- They simply don't have the time to make it an important thing
- They are annoyed with me and participate reluctantly

5. When you have sex, how do you feel?

- I feel very close to my partner
- I'm happy, but sometimes I want to do something new
- Bored and not connected with my spouse at all

6. What is the biggest problem you have with your sex life right now?

- Daily living and life's stresses taking over
- Not being possible to have enough private time at home
- My partner is rarely up to it or available

Now, think about your answers. Is there something you can do differently to change the situation if needed? Arrange for some quiet time with your spouse, and discuss both your answers to this quiz.

Intimacy and our sex lives are mostly a topic that we are reluctant to discuss. It takes confidence to discuss the most personal matters with your spouse. However, like other aspects of your relationship, it is crucial to be honest about intercourse, your feelings, and your needs, and it is essential to compromise where needed.

Chapter 5
Mega Millions

Were you ever confronted with a basic question about your spouse and couldn't find the answer? Is it lunch or sweets that they tend to prefer? We've come up with a brilliant plan to get you involved! Our Mega Millions lottery game is the ideal approach to discovering what your partner is currently fascinated with! Favorite things vary throughout time, so even if you used to remember all of your spouse's preferences, many of the responses are sure to have changed. You take in everything your sweetheart says when you're in a new relationship. The previously absorbed data has most likely become outdated as time has passed. No worries, though; this game will help you out (and get you out of trouble!)

Win the Couples Lotto

Complete the lotto with your partner's preferred 5+1 winning numbers. Their first option should be "plus 1," then the following five answers. The chances of winning the lottery are incredibly slim, so make sure you guarantee a large prize to your spouse if they do!

Compare your responses to those of your spouse. You will receive 5 points for each accurate "plus 1" value and 1 point for each other's correct number.

No 1	Favorite Food
1. Pizza 2. Chicken burger 3. Spaghetti and meatballs 4. Vegetable lasagna 5. Turkey pie 6. Steak and fries 7. Beef burger 8. Pasta alfredo	9. Green salad 10. Toasted cheese sandwich 11. Sausage roll 12. Corn dog 13. Apple pie 14. Ice-cream 15. Seafood 16. Fish & chips 17. Bacon, eggs & toast

Numbers

No 2	Favorite Pizza topping?
1.Pepperoni 2.Mushroom 3.Extra cheese 4.Sausage 5.Onion 6.Black olives 7.Green pepper	8.Fresh garlic 9.Tomato 10.Fresh basil 11.Pineapple 12.Bacon 13.Seafood 14.Minced beef

Numbers

No 3	Favorite Music Genre?
1. Rock 2. Pop 3. Heavy metal 4. Jazz 5. Electronic dance music 6. Alternative rock 7. Classical music 8. Hip hop 9. Contemporary	10. Punk rock 11. Pop-rock 12. Blues 13. Folk music 14. Blues 15. Country 16. World music 17. Indie rock music 18. Soul music

Numbers

No 4	Favorite country you want to visit?
1. France 2. Canada 3. Switzerland 4. Australia 5. New Zealand 6. USA 7. China 8. Spain 9. Germany 10. Japan	11. South Africa 12. India 13. Sweden 14. Netherlands 15. Norway 16. Denmark 17. England 18. Ireland 19. Scotland

Numbers

No 5	Favorite sport?
1. Football 2. Cricket 3. Soccer 4. Hockey 5. Tennis 6. Rugby	7. Baseball 8. Basketball 9. Volleyball 10. Table tennis 11. Golf 12. Swimming

Numbers

No 6	Favorite way to relax?
1. Play video games 2. Get active 3. Take deep breaths 4. Listen to music 5. Stock up on chocolate 6. Have a hug	7. Pamper yourself 8. Have a laugh 9. Watch movies or a TV series 10. Watch YouTube videos 11. Drink coffee 12. Sleep

Numbers

No 7	Favorite comfort food?
1. Waffles 2. Flapjacks 3. Spaghetti and meatballs 4. Fried chicken 5. Mac and cheese 6. Pizza	7. Hamburger 8. French fries 9. Ice cream 10. Chocolate 11. Cake 12. Biscuits

Numbers

No 8	Favorite Pasta Dish?
1. Spaghetti bolognese 2. Lasagna 3. Fettuccine alfredo 4. Pasta carbonara	5. Ravioli 6. Pasta alla Norma 7. Spaghetti alle Vongole 8. Macaroni and cheese 9. Pasta and steak
Numbers	

No 9	Favorite Wild Animal?
1. Lion 2. Cheetah 3. Leopard 4. Elephant 5. Bear 6. Tortoise 7. Hyena	8. Wolf 9. Zebra 10. Buffalo 11. Rhino 12. Hippopotamus 13. Crocodile 14. Alligator
Numbers	

No 10	Favorite Color?
1. Blue 2. Green 3. Black 4. Red 5. Orange 6. Purple 7. Yellow	8. Gold 9. White 10. Silver 11. Pink 12. Charcoal 13. Gray 14. Sky blue
Numbers	

Winning Together: Deal With Anger

Important steps for many spouses at the start of a relationship are to get to a point at which they can be open to the potential of transformation and be honest with their spouse. A good relationship does not always seem 'natural' at first. Whenever a kid has experienced trauma, abandonment, or abuse as a youngster, the road to recovery may include moments of acute agony and fear (Muñoz).

Access to an underlying basis of "secure connection" isn't a given, as per Amir Levine and Rachel Heller's book, titled *Attached*. According to statistics, just 50% of the nation is "tightly connected." It should be deserved and fought for by the remainder among us.

This chapter is for spouses who want to work on arguing less and loving each other more in a practical, inexpensive, and long-term approach. The challenges, advice, and prompts offered here are supposed to be spontaneous, relevant, and appropriate for wherever you may be in your lifetime. I recommend choosing a physical and/or psychological "Lovers Zone" before beginning the activities. This is where you will meet to discuss the mission. You may either select an actual spot in your house, a virtual spot if you're in different physical places or just change into a clear, inquiring mindset.

It might be challenging to communicate with our spouses. When it comes to sensitive matters, the risks of fighting are frequently higher. In this chapter, I challenge you to try something new: Talk to your spouse about difficult topics on a constant basis. I'm encouraging you to confront sensitive situations face-on instead of waiting for it to catch you off guard. Make time for each other by spending roughly 20 minutes each week working on your relationship.

Exercise 1

Taking turns, the one assigned to speak selects some of their favorite bad stories (common "Scary Stories" list below), then describes how these stories commonly arise in their relationships. How do you perceive yourself, your spouse, and your marriage if you believe these narratives? How do you deal with it or respond to it (Muñoz)?

SCARY STORIES LIST

- I'm not enough.
- I'm not a likable person.
- I can't get things right.
- I'm too old to fall in love.
- I'm shattered. I don't have any faith in people.
- I have no support in this world.
- I don't belong here.
- You don't care about me.
- I'm destined to fail.
- Everyone has deserted me.
- My wants are unimportant.
- I'm a tad too much for other people.
- I'll never be happy.
- I'm totally worthless.
- People use me.

SAMPLE

Communicator Spouse: One of my worst marriage nightmares is that I can't do anything properly. For example: When you ask in an irritated tone where I placed the vehicle keys, I tell myself this. It makes me feel disheartened and incompetent. I deal by withholding affection and convincing myself of additional scary scenarios, such as how we'll never be able to make it as a team. I get furious and sad when I choose to believe such things. I relax by getting myself a drink of whiskey or browsing the web for hours.

Listening Spouse: Thank you for acknowledging and confessing to your relationship trauma experiences. It makes us realize that they're simply ideas and that they shouldn't have to drive our relationship.

Exercise 2

Communicator Spouse:

Taking turns as speaker and listener, both partners spend a bit of time highlighting one item from the "List of Offenses" that they can't stand or try coming up with their very own offenses. The speaking spouse explains their strongest offense viewpoint and why it is so important to them. The speaker next flips the perspective and considers how the opposite is the case. How would it feel to do something like this? What would it be like to let go of the desire to prove your viewpoint in a disagreement with your spouse?

List of Offenses

- Always provide a helping hand to those in need.
- Always maintain a courteous demeanor.
- If you care about me, you care about the things I care about.
- It is critical to arrive on time.
- It's all about having a good time.
- It is unforgivable to lie.
- You make someone feel significant when you adore them.
- Relaxing and letting go is not a good idea.
- You disclose all your vulnerabilities in a strong relationship.
- You'll remember what's essential to me if you truly love me.
- When I'm unwell, you should look after me.
- You should hold our troubles to yourself as it is private.
- If you're feeling very giving, you may insist on paying.
- It is necessary to remember all anniversaries.

Example:

Communicator Spouse: "Life is about enjoyment," I picked as my philosophy. I become concerned when marriages cease being fun and cheerful and become weighed down by hefty emotions and talks. I've constantly battled with the concept that "Life is about having a great time" since I believe that immediately when you get too sentimental or too serious, you're on the road to unhappiness. "Life is not about having a great time" or "Life is serious" are the polar opposites of this idea. So I can see how this may be the case. Life may be difficult and unforeseen. When I think about it, it saddens me greatly. Perhaps that's why I want my existence to be all about having fun and not having to work. I despise being depressed.

Spouse Who Actively Listens: Thank you for sharing one of your views with me and for being open to the possibility that the opposing opinion might be just as real as the one you feel is correct.

Stop the Argument Before It Gets Out of Hand

On her website, the couples therapist, Alicia Muñoz, shares a method to halt an argument before it spirals out of control.

She shares a conflict-stopping approach that will help you reinvent peace with your spouse, even if you're in the thick of a quarrel. The more you apply and practice this approach, the more it will help you. It's what Muñoz refers to as the "'Take Two" method.

"Take Twos" are straightforward to do (although not always easy). Before you start attempting these, you'll need your spouse's approval, so discuss it ahead of time and modify it to your needs. Perhaps share this post with a friend and develop a plan to test one out in a brief fight.

The following is how it tends to work: Stop fighting as soon as you recognize it has begun. If needed, interrupt in the middle of a phrase. Say to your spouse, "Let's do a Take-Two."

Replay the 'scene' of your fight from the time you were provoked if your spouse agrees, and you've both taken a few deep breaths. Pick the first trigger point you can recall if there are numerous. Then, start over the scene. Do something new this time—even if it's only a tiny bit different. Consider the following scenario:

- Use feeling words and 'I' language instead of judging or condemning. Avoid 'we' language.
- Rather than sniping or discarding each other, turn to each other with an open mind.
- Your body posture and facial expressions should reflect your sincerity.
- Use an endearing phrase.
- Take ownership of your emotions, ideas, and responses.

Don't be concerned about seeming 'real.' It's pretty okay to feel clumsy or awkward. Simply do it in a highly 'relational' manner. "Take Two" succeeds even if they appear hurried or 'cliched. ' In truth, just disengaging from the initial 'take' of your disagreement demonstrates that you're prepared to accept responsibility for your role in encouraging the divide with your spouse. This activity is about accepting responsibility for your role in a conflict, allowing yourself and your spouse a second opportunity, resisting the need to protect or blame, and reacting in a positive way. Kindness is not the same for everyone. In terms of relationships, things work differently.

Chapter 6
Fun! Part Two

A happy marriage contains experiences that help you create beautiful memories, make you giggle, bring you closer, and express your feelings for one another in unspoken ways. The following are a few excellent suggestions to avoid being imprisoned in a tedious, everyday schedule to get you thinking about exciting new experiences instead.

Bring Sexy Back - Playing Games to Encourage Intimacy

Here are some of the best romantic and funny partner games that you both should try to add spark and magic to your relationship:

Roulette for Two or Doubles

You need two glasses of wine, preferably, to play this. It is not necessary, however, that the beverage be alcoholic. You can simply grab your favorite fizzy drink if you don't want to drink.

One will pose a question to the other partner in the game, and both of you will respond with a 'yes' or 'no.' This will continue until the game is over. It can also be played as a double date game if preferred.

The Ship Sinking Game

The "Ship Sinking Game" is a fun activity that is particularly popular among lovers. This requires that your drink (a shot glass) be topped with enough liquid to allow it to float in a bigger glass of liquid. The idea is to keep the shot glass from sinking into the larger glass containing it. The one who loses will be forced to comply with the wishes of their loved one.

The Fundamental One (Truth or Dare)

Don't want to play it with a lot of people around you? Not an issue! Allow yourself and your companion to take pleasure in it. If they select 'truth,' you may ask private or humorous questions and add some pressure if they prefer the dare option over the truth option. Play two truths and one lie at the same time. It is the couples' turn to play this game, in which they each state two correct facts and one incorrect fact about themselves. The other spouse needs to figure out what is true and what is not.

Do a Scavenger Hunt

Prepare for a search, and leave a few lovely notes to point your spouse to the amazing surprise you've planned for them in advance of the search. The surprise might be anything from a watch to a romantic supper by candlelight—or it could even be you!

Prep Challenges

There is a method to make the game more thrilling by putting a time restriction on it, as well as other options. Find out who is the most efficient or superior chef. You may also transform this game into a pretzel-eating contest if you like, in order to consume pretzels rather than prepare them.

Deal or No Deal

Playing this well-known cash game may be a romantic experience that can be taken to a whole new level of intimacy. A slight adjustment might transform this routine game for your spouse into a more enjoyable and exciting experience. Lay down a large cash envelope in front of your spouse, along with your romantic desire, and let them choose which one they want.

Craft Some Origami

Japanese paper crafts could be lots of fun to do as a couple! Choose from the many YouTube videos available and collaborate on them with a friend or family member. All you'll need is a package of brightly colored sheets. You may make it into a fun game by playing with your friends or by making it a competition (within a reasonable time limit).

Tic-Tac-Toe

Take a stack of paper sheets and draw cards from them to illustrate intimate behaviors. Take another piece of paper and draw different boxes to illustrate various concepts, such as kissing, snuggling, and so on. When you and your opponent have decided on a position, you must both accomplish the action that has been specified, and then the following turn is played. Anyone who wins a round (completely) will expect something in return from their opponent!

One, Two, Stare at You

Within a staring contest, there is an element of intimacy. Your spouse may not be willing to participate in this contest if you expressly request it. Simply fix your gaze on theirs, and you'll be fine. Don't say anything at all; enjoy the present time as a couple. Continue to stare into their eyes with affection. If you give it another shot later, you'll be grateful for this book.

The 'I Spy With My Little Eye' Challenge

This is a popular game among children. You can snuggle up with a buddy and attempt to find things in a book, or you can get in your vehicle and go someplace. It may be anywhere, including a park or a shop. Afterward, take turns in providing each other with clues as to what you are seeing. It's a fun game to play when you and your partner go on a road trip together.

Ding Dong Ditch

Ding Dong Ditch is an ancient adage. To be sure, you're going to ring doorbells and dash away before anybody answers the door, but you're also going to leave a goodie behind to surprise folks. It'll be a fun Halloween or Christmas game to play with your significant other, and it can be played anywhere.

Home-Made Charades

Play a game of self-invented charades. Only you and your partner have the ability to include personal hints. The indications might consist of things like favorite programs, inside jokes, terms you use a lot, and things you have in common.

Try Various Types of Card Games

The use of nontraditional kinds of cards is common in many popular card games, such as Poker, War, Blackjack, and Slapjack, even though these games are played with standard types of cards. Listed below are some entertaining card games you and your companion may play on a date night: Uno, Five, Monopoly Deal, Set, and Crowns.

The One That Is the Most Personal (Role-Play)

In order to make it more fascinating, you should strive to dress in the manner of the persona you are supposed to represent. Always try to imitate or behave the same way as them and adopt their words and mannerisms. It is also an excellent method of improving your sex life.

Experiment With a Variety of Board Games

Mancala, Yahtzee, Clue, Stratego, Hive, Flash, Burgundy Castles, Scrabble, Checkers, Trivial Pursuit, Life, Exploding Kittens, Ticket to Ride, Dominion, and Carcassonne are just a few of the two-player games that may be played on dating evenings with your spouse.

The Most Iconic Figures of This Time Period (Video Games)

A single person often plays these games, but they may be much more fun when played as a pair. Here's a compilation you and your loved one should enjoy: Video games such as World of Warcraft, Brawl, Super Smash Bros, Halo, Snipperclips, Bomberman, Diablo, and Rock Band are examples of what you may find. Other examples include Lego games, Overcooked, Mario Kart, Mario Party, and Minecraft (Holme).

More Fun Interactive Games

Love is triggered when the right part of the brain is touched in the right place. For example, when the parts of the brain that are responsible for imagination, creativity, and curiosity are activated, you feel the excitement associated with intrigue and possibility. Then, just picture what occurs when you fantasize about your lover in the most appropriate manner possible. So, to further awaken those feelings, it is necessary to play many interactive, fun games as a couple (Sytner).

Famous Couples from Literature, History, and Art Game

1. Prince Phillip / _____ / a. Lady Bird

2. Jim Halpert / _____ / b. Buttercup

3. Adam / _____ / c. Jane Porter

4. Clark Kent / _____ / d. Elizabeth Bennet

5. Johnny Cash / _____ / e. Ariel

6. George / _____ / f. Juliet

7. John Lennon / _____ / g. Wilma

8. Wesley / _____ / h. Aurora

9. Peeta Melark / _____ / i. Sarah

10. Han Solo / _____ / j. Olive Oyl

11. Popeye / _____ / k. Miss Piggy

12. Mr. Darcy / _____ / l. Priscilla

13. Prince William / _____ / m. Mary Jane Watson

14. Abraham / _____ / n. Pam Beasley

15. Ricky Ricardo / _____ / o. Mindy

16. LBJ / _____ / p. Kate Middleton

17. Kermit / _____ / q. Helen Parr

18. Romeo / _____ / r. Princess Leia

19. Mork / _____ / s. Jackie

20. Aquila / _____ / t. Eve

21. Prince Eric / _____ / u. June Carter

22. Fred Flintstone / _____ / v. Katniss Everdeen

23. JFK / _____ / w. Yoko Ono

24. Tarzan / _____ / x. Lucille Ball

25. Mr. Incredible / _____ / y. Lois Lane

26. Peter Parker / _____ / z. Martha

Once done, check for answers here.

Word Search: Emotions in Relationships

T	R	E	T	H	G	U	A	L	H
G	R	A	I	L	I	M	A	F	O
G	N	O	F	L	H	H	P	S	N
O	R	I	F	G	O	V	V	I	E
K	N	A	V	F	P	B	N	L	S
G	L	E	C	I	E	N	F	L	T
I	O	S	N	I	G	G	U	Y	R
S	V	P	A	E	O	R	D	F	U
J	E	T	P	F	S	U	O	V	T
K	I	N	D	N	E	S	S	F	H

Word Chest:

Effort	Fun	Familiar	Forgiving
Honest	Gracious	Kindness	Hope
Laughter	Safe	Love	Silly
	Oneness	Truth	

Check your answers on page 155.

Get Yourself Some Fake Identities Game

The supplies required are as follows:

- Props or a disguise
- Using a pen or a pencil

79

Timeline: One to two hours

You may add some spice to your relationship by pretending to be a completely different pair for a short period of time or by pretending to be two complete strangers. You're not re-meeting each other here; you're entirely reinventing your lives. It is all up to you! Polish up on your performing talents as a couple and learn to view one another in a whole new light. What adventures are in store for you if you follow your dreams?

How to Play:

Pretend you're superheroes or famous people, or pretend you're characters from your favorite fictional novels or movies. You don't have to choose people who are (or have been) in a relationship, so famous couples and romance aren't required. Perhaps Elizabeth Bennet will get the opportunity to meet Abraham Lincoln. What would be the outcome of such a conversation? There is nobody who is off-bounds. Go on a date, run errands together, or spend time at home, but only communicate with each other as your characters. Some intriguing (and sometimes humorous) discussions will result from this.

Tip:

If you find yourself participating in this exercise multiple times, make notes each time you do so. Years from now, you could find yourself having a notebook full of crazy, humorous tales to share or appreciate with your family and friends (Schwanke).

Chapter 7
Communication

There are highs and lows to being in a marriage. It's the same with starting a family. When it comes to conflict, it is well acknowledged that communication may strongly influence any relationship's progress (or the lack thereof). While the phrase "better and quicker" has become ingrained in many public messaging, it may not be the most incredible method to develop a good relationship. Couples may repeat some activities so frequently that they operate more on autopilot than on purpose—which, although fantastic for aircraft, is a nightmare for relationships. Our minds frequently wander away from the present moment, making it harder to reach the appropriate level of intimacy in our marriages. Contrary to popular belief, slowing down improves general well-being, including relationship satisfaction. Couples may slow it down by practicing mindfulness, which focuses on self-reflection, awareness, non-criticism, and a characteristic of being present (Leavitt).

Did you know that one out of every three marriages in the United States results in divorce? Loneliness, exhaustion, failure to communicate, loss of intimate connection, and pressure are all elements that contribute to the probability of a successful marriage in today's fast culture. If you're having trouble with some of those, relaxation techniques are a great way to improve your marriage fulfillment.

Quick Communication Tips to Get You Thinking About the Topic You Are About to Embrace:

- Give them some space.
- Talk to each other in person, face-to-face.
- Use "I" statements when things go wrong.
- Be completely honest.
- Chat about the small stuff.
- Make sure to follow the 24-hour cool-down rule.
- Maintain personal contact (hugs, hands, touch, kiss).
- The best way to make interaction fun is to make it interesting.

This chapter will help you with adding some fun to your marriage.

Relaxation Techniques

Life is sure to be challenging at some points. First of all, getting some alone time after a stressful day or week is one of the finest techniques to reclaim your sanity. Finding methods to be with each other while still relaxing is critical when you're in a relationship. Here are some practical suggestions for reducing stress levels with your best person on the planet. Relaxation techniques for couples explain how couples can de-stress together in many ways (Malacoff). Let's have a look at some of these ways.

Have a Dinner Without Using Your Phone

A meal without mobile phones, whether at home or when you're in public, may do wonders for your mood. It may seem easy, but you'd be surprised how many people allow their devices to be a constant source of distraction throughout their day. Reconnect during a quiet and romantic supper with your cell phone switched off. Because there will be no distractions, excellent discussion and quiet time will flourish.

Take a Yoga Class

Yoga has a natural calming effect. So, why don't you try it as a pair? Go to a class, or if you're not so confident, set up your mats in the privacy of your own house!

Make a Visit to a Comedy Club

Laughter is equally as vital as food and nourishment to your lifestyle. Laughter is effective stress, pain, and conflict reliever. Laughter improves immunity, boosts metabolism, and releases endorphins. Couples should make an effort to include humor in their time spent together. Visiting comedy clubs, going to movie nights, or even telling knock-knock jokes should suffice.

Play a Board Game

Whichever games you like, sitting back and enjoying a couple of hours playing them with your spouse is a great way to bond and escape from the hassles of daily life.

Binge-Watch a Heartwarming TV Show or Film

Binge-watch a meaningful series or watch a movie. This may seem ridiculous, but sometimes all you need is a decent cry to relieve tension and remember what's essential in life.

Consider a Staycation

Although a lavish trip may appear to be the ideal way to unwind, this may not be attainable. Alternatively, why not take a staycation? The majority of individuals do not take advantage of all of the great things that their own beautiful city has to offer. An overnight staycation in your backyard might help you relax by providing excitement and the opportunity to try something different. However, if you're looking for a full-fledged vacation, try taking a weekend trip.

Have a Secret Slumber

Set out time to reconnect as a couple. Not only does the secret addition to the thrill and suspense, but the Mayo Clinic also claims that taking a quick rest (30 minutes) can improve alertness, emotions, cognition, and productivity.

Listen to Each Other While Lying Down

Listening to one another may be the best thing you can do as a unit. Asking your spouse to unload and express all that got them stirred up from the start is a terrific way to get them to relax completely. Once you've gotten all of the outside noise off your shoulders, you'll be able to place it beside you and start from scratch with new ideas and thoughts.

Take a Bath Together

This one is traditional, but that doesn't mean it's not valid. Filling up the tub with a bubble bath or a scented bath bomb and enjoying a soak around each other are not only sensual but also enjoyable.

Consider a Couples Massage

Getting a foot or a complete body massage with your spouse on a bed next to you is bonding and calming. If the weather cooperates, have the rub-down outside to give a different physical sensation to the equation. If your budget does not allow for a specialist masseuse, you may do it yourself by massaging one another.

Take a Stroll

A comfy sofa and television are typically the first things that spring to your mind when thinking of ways to unwind, but there is a benefit to be gained by going on a stroll as a couple. "To be in nature affects our physiological nature spontaneously, which can have a favorable influence on our morale'.

When You Go to Bed, Go Together

The benefit of being in bed with your spouse cannot be overlooked. Couples who do not go to bed together lose connection and closeness. Partners who do not go to bed at the same time waste considerable time in which they could be having significant chats, doing common hobbies, and having sex. The time spent in bed preceding sleeping might really be one of the most restful. In fact, studies suggest that cuddling time makes partners feel better loved and relaxed.

48 Hours of Ghosting

We live in an age of sensory overload, and most of us hardly get the chance to disengage from the rest of the world. It's time to switch off: Place your smartphones in a sealed bag and reconnect with your spouse on an intimate level with no interruptions and some good old-fashioned talk. If you're anxious about crises at home or at work, check your phone once in a while to see if there are any urgent missed calls or messages.

Meditate as Much as You Can

Meditation has been linked to calmness, focus, and a variety of other benefits that promote a calm and balanced mentality. Even if it's commonly seen as a personal activity, it may be done jointly to bring connection and intimacy to your marriage.

Take a Couples Retreat

A couples retreat is ideal for couples who need reconnection. It's a great way to spend quality time with your significant other. Go on a couples retreat if you and your partner need a connection boost. There are a variety of retreats to choose from, including outdoor retreats, romantic retreats, and more. You'll not only be able to relax and feel more content in your relationship, but you'll also be able to meet other couples who are on the same route.

Have Fun With Your Dog

Because most animals love their owners unconditionally, bringing your dog out to run around and play is sure to be a happy moment. Don't have a pet? Check with a buddy to see if you can borrow one for the day or visit a shelter where you and your spouse can play with the dogs.

Play or Listen to Some Music

It doesn't matter if you're in the vehicle, at home, or at a performance (whether you're in the audience or the performers). Allow the music to do its magic as you listen to something you mutually enjoy.

Stargazing at the Night Sky

Cuddled up, being silent, and gazing up at the night sky may be incredibly pleasant, whether it's chilly or warmer outside. Take a blanket and a snack, and simply enjoy one another's companionship. Sometimes, it's good to see each other in a beautiful place and be really quiet.

Grow a Garden of Tranquility

Combine forces and help create an indoor herb garden or an outdoor food patch. Choosing what to produce, caring for your seedlings, and working out how to prepare your harvest can give you hours of tension-free quality time.

Go Shopping Together for Something You Both Want

Set aside some money and go shopping for something that will offer you equal delight, whether it's a new car, a gourmet coffee machine, or a bigger television screen.

Dance Away Your Troubles

Take a class, go to a nightclub, or listen to music privately. Like other types of exercise, dancing produces endorphins, giving your brain and body a good sensation.

Consider Joining a Fitness Class Together

Working out as a team is a great way to relax, but if you want to change it up differently, ditch the treadmill, and sign up for a class that neither of you has previously tried. The possibilities are unlimited, be it spinning, yoga, bootcamp, or CrossFit.

Take a Break After Work With Your Spouse

The feeling that your spouse is there for you is among the most significant components of a marriage. There is a chance to unwind together while we move from work to home life: Slip into comfy clothing, take off our shoes, and perhaps enjoy a couple of glasses of wine or cups of coffee. Here, active listening and open conversation are crucial.

Break the Routine However You Want To

Make sure anything you do to relax with your spouse is unique from what you usually do. Break free from your usual schedule. Breaking the routine is vital for your marriage, whether you go for a walk on the beach or stay at an exotic guesthouse.

Mindfulness and Communication Methods

It's impossible to work on your marriage and improve your communication abilities in the spur of the moment. Committing to these activities is a worthwhile effort that will result in a deeper, closer relationship.

Consider the following before doing any of the activities listed:

- Find a peaceful, diversion-free location away from children or work.
- Make a promise to one another that you will approach these activities with a good mindset.
- Even if an activity feels uncomfortable or silly, try it nonetheless. What you discover about each other can amaze you.
- If you find a problem that irritates one or both of you, go to a different activity and work through the issue with a couple's therapist.
- Write notes or keep a diary about how these activities improved your marriage.

Are you ready to begin? Here are a few enjoyable and insightful relationship activities for partners' communication (Davenport).

Have an Honest Talk With Your Spouse

The term "Fireside Talk" has symbolized love, accessibility, and an open-to-say-anything attitude since President Roosevelt first hosted these to engage with the American people, giving his lectures the very nickname of "fireside chats," to suggest the picture of a pleasant discussion with the government in front of a blazing fire.

So choose a comfy seat for each of you, get a lovely drink for the both of you, and settle down for a friendly talk. Give one another your full attention, and be willing to voice everything that's on your mind.

Refocus, Remorse, and Repair

We all have a past, and it doesn't take long in a romantic relationship for one of you to say something that offends, criticizes, or devalues the other in whatever manner. Take some time for each of you to quietly bring up one painful comment or offense made by the other so that you may both work on rewording the meaning behind those remarks in a more caring manner. This exercise is designed to create a safe environment for coping with old wounds that one or both of you are currently struggling to move over or get over. The person who made the remark now has the opportunity to communicate their dissatisfaction or frustration in a different manner while offering a genuine apology for the hurt caused by the way it was addressed.

Take Turns Speaking (Use a Timer)

Establishing time limitations and allowing each party to talk without interference from the other might be beneficial. If it's your time to listen, so avoid the need to justify or make explanations for anything you said or did that upset or irritated the other person. You can also take turns discussing the highlights of your day and a single event that brought you down a notch during the day. If it's your turn to listen, wordless expressions can communicate support, empathy, and compassion—but keep your mouth shut until your spouse's turn is over. Between turns, you can each think about what the other has said. During these sessions, both parties are permitted to speak.

Create an "Us" Notebook

Take turns penning notes to each other in a notebook that you both feel comfortable writing in. This diary may be used for spontaneous love letters, expressing gratitude about a thing, or expressing a strong feeling about a matter without accusing or condemning the other person. Consider how your spouse will react to your comments and attempt to express yourself in a way that does not exclude or set the other on the defensive. Instead of keeping a collaborative diary, you might write letters to each other. Any of these methods will not only increase your couple's communicative abilities overall but will also improve your writing skills, which can only be beneficial to both of you.

Find Out Each Other's Love Languages and Act Accordingly

Are you familiar with Dr. Gary Chapman's book, *The Five Love Languages*? According to Chapman, each love language expresses how we like to express and receive love. Words of affirmation, acts of service, accepting gifts, memorable moments spent together, and physical contact is examples of all these. Offer one another at least three distinct alternatives for a couple's treat, using at least three different love languages in the process. For instance, one of you may offer the following options to the other: An extended embrace and a neck rub (or back massage), or perhaps a chance to spend at least 30 minutes with your spouse's entire focus. While one is cleaning the kitchen, the other can take a nice bath. A meaningful surprise or gift based on what you know about your spouse would also be nice. Sincere, authentic words of praise, too, are a great option. The list goes on. The more you do this exercise, the better you will start understanding each other's love languages and needs to enable you to fuel each other's love tanks.

Talk About Your Future Objectives and Dreams

If you're married, it's crucial that you both understand one other's objectives and what you want to achieve in your lives and in the next five years. Respond to the following issues as a couple: What do you truly desire? What makes you think you'd like that? What can your spouse do to assist you? This may appear to be a one-time occurrence; however, it's not. Priorities may shift, and the more you grow as a couple, the more likely you will allow yourself to be driven by instinct rather than purpose. Also, the more you know about each other's objectives and aspirations, the more bonded you'll feel, and the better you'll know each other.

Share Phrases in Your Favorite Songs

Even if this may seem like one of those cliché communication games for married couples, this is, in fact, a fun activity that improves your knowledge about your spouse.

Pick at least one song each that you feel applies to you, and recite the lyrics that are most meaningful to you. Ever had trouble expressing your thoughts, but then you heard a song that translated the chaotic mess in your heart? Share that song with your loved one.

Discuss why this song fits the bill, and see if you can connect the lyrics to a memory from your own life. The goal is to gain an understanding of how your spouse thinks and why specific music phrases are significant to him or her. You may play the music for each other and carefully listen to one another's selections.

Maybe it won't become one of your favorites, but from then on, every time you hear that song, you'll think of your beloved and of the time they shared the song with you.

Share Eye Contact While Being Still

For five minutes, sit and make unbroken eye contact with each other without saying anything. You can communicate nonverbally, but don't talk or make any sounds until the timer goes off. Following that, you may talk about how it felt for you, what was going through your mind, and what you believed the other one was contemplating (based on nonverbal interpretation and what you know about your spouse).

Sit facing each other if it helps. If looking into one another's eyes becomes too much for one of you, press your foreheads together and just enjoy the contact quietly.

Play the Name Game

You and your partner must think of a famous celebrity and write their name down on a post-it note. Your spouse should put your post-it note on their head.

Then, each person asks a closed (yes/no) question. There is no limit to how many times you can ask questions, so long as you get a 'yes' response. No? Then switch. For example, here are some common ones:

- Am I still alive?
- Am I a woman?
- Do I play sports?
- Do I act?

It's time to stop the game after ten minutes. Now, your spouse may place their post-it note on your head, and it's your turn to ask questions and guess who you are.

Practice Active and Empathic Listening

Do you find yourself subconsciously preparing what you want to say while also listening to your spouse speak? Are you maybe just waiting for them to finish so you can provide your viewpoint or defend yourself? With attentive listening, you observe with the primary purpose of hearing what your spouse has to say while also attempting to comprehend their intent and sentiments. You repeat back to your spouse what you noticed them say to make sure you got it right.

Empathic, active listening is a type of listening that goes a step beyond. Compassionate listening necessitates putting yourself in your partner's position and seeing events through their eyes.

Start Using the "I" Instead of "You" Statements

When speaking with your spouse about a problem you're having, it's natural to tell them what it is they're doing wrong that's bothering you. "You leave me feeling foolish when you speak to me like that," you could add. Taking cheap shots of guilt at your spouse, on the other hand, is likely to make them reactive and upset. Instead of expressing what they are doing that upsets you, you should express how their words or actions cause you to feel. Use non-triggering "I" sentences, such as "I feel foolish when you tell me how to clean the kitchen." Take control of your emotions and request your spouse's affection, as well as supporting phrases and acts.

Concentrate on Compassion and Mutual Respect

Keeping cool during disagreements is challenging, and avoiding saying things you regret. Feelings of resentment and fury might cause us to break out in cruel ways, destroying your close bond and mutual understanding.

According to Dr. John Gottman, a relationship specialist, and author, it takes five pleasant contacts with your spouse to mend one bad experience. Why would you put yourself in such a situation? Practice communicating to your spouse with love and respect throughout all situations, including tense and challenging ones. Recognize the risk you are placing your marriage in by saying and doing bad stuff and make it your mission to prioritize compassion.

Share Your Story With Your Spouse

Take turns sharing with each other a key event from your past. It may be something extraordinary or perhaps something painful or difficult to discuss. Give as much information as you can, explaining why the event is significant to you and how the experience affected you. The listener must start reflecting on what they experienced throughout the story's delivery.

- What are all the key points in your spouse's story?
- What feelings did your spouse convey?
- What sections of the story triggered such emotional reactions?

- How has your spouse been affected by the shared circumstances?

This practice helps you focus on conveying your emotions and listening to each other from your heart. Don't pass judgment if your spouse refuses to address some of these topics.

The Sandwich Method

When it comes to truth and marriage, it's often easier said than done. Although you want to tell your spouse the truth or help them with the truth, sometimes the way you convey the message makes things worse, or sometimes you may prefer not to say anything because you are scared of the conflict that it may cause, and this in turn only worsens the problem. What if I told you that there was actually a strategy to help you tell the truth and convey the message in a peaceful manner that won't result in conflict? Because there is, it is called the "sandwich method." How can a sandwich method help you, though, and what does it entail?

The sandwich method is a communication approach that may help you be so much more authoritative while still sparing some sentiments (Campbell). Use this phrase when providing honest feedback or trying to persuade someone to adjust their conduct. It can assist you in lessening the blow to anyone's pride. You may use this with relationships, spouses, fellow employees, colleagues, or anybody else with whom you have a lasting connection. But keep in mind that if you're actually coming from a good position and the other person isn't, they may still become angry, and that's on them. Their reaction is their own choice. The sandwich method consists of the following three steps: Start with a positive statement. For example, "Thank you for picking up the kids from school today." Then, slip in the negative, for example: "Will you also be able to pick them up tomorrow? Finish off your request with the top of your sandwich—something positive again, for example: "Thank you, that would be fantastic, it would help me so much!"

Expressing Gratitude

Think of your latest conversation with your spouse—was it this morning when you woke up and you were talking about who would prepare breakfast or drop the kids off—or maybe in the afternoon, with a quick conversation about who would be buying the milk or what would you be having for dinner? Whatever the details may be of your last interaction with each other, the chance may be high that it was a casual conversation. When was the last time you actually had a conversation with your spouse centered on complimenting them, telling them how wonderful they are, how much you appreciate them, that they are worthy and that you see all the hard work that they are doing for your family? I suppose this isn't the usual type of conversation we are having on a daily basis. Life is so overwhelming and full of scheduled business, but if you think about it, is this not precisely the only type of conversation we should be having? Life is so short, and it can end for any of us at any moment. Don't we want to compliment and tell each other what we mean to one another before we run out of time?

If you want to compliment your spouse but you don't know how or where to start, read on. We have already spoken about Dr. Chapman's love languages, but what if you can base your actions on their specific love language to show your partner gratitude (Daly)? The way you give and receive love may be based on your particular love language. Whether your partner prefers words of affirmation, receiving gifts, quality time, acts of service, or physical touch, this may guide you to choose a way to show gratitude to them. For example, if your partner prefers words of affirmation, you may write them a love letter, or if they like receiving gifts, you may buy them chocolate or give them a bunch of flowers. If they prefer quality time, arrange a picnic and spend the afternoon with them. If they prefer acts of service, allow them to go and enjoy a bath while you do the dishes. Tell them why you are doing this or have given it to them, to show them how much you love them, and to thank them for all they do for you daily. Also, tell them that although you know that this is only a small token, you really want them to know how much you value them.

Stress-Reducing Conversations

The technique to have a stress-reducing chat or conversation is actually simply based on active and compassionate listening, according to Ellie Lisitsa, an editor for The Gottman Relationship Blog (Lisitsa). Here are some simple steps to having a stress-relieving discussion. Rely on insights from the following exercise as you tackle the "How was your day, dear?" topic from a different angle.

This exercise is based on the practice of "active listening," which aims to have you listen (rather than merely hear) to the subject's words with empathy and without criticism. If you don't believe your spouse is attentive to you, you won't be feeling emotionally attracted to them. When the technique is used in couples therapy, it frequently fails because pairs are required to utilize it when voicing their grievances with one another, and if they do not know how to listen actively, it slows down the process of resolving issues.

However, this listening strategy may be incredibly effective if used explicitly during talks in which you are not your partner's target. In this setting, you'll be considerably more open to being helpful and supportive of your spouse, thereby building mutual trust and love. Here are eight ground principles for having this conversation:

1. Make turns to complain. Each spouse gets the opportunity to be the complainer for a predetermined time frame.
2. Don't make unwanted suggestions. When it comes to assisting your spouse in de-stressing, the most important guideline to remember is that empathy must come before suggestions.
3. Display real interest. Do not even allow your thoughts or eyes to stray. Try to keep your attention on your partner.
4. Express your support. Let your spouse know you understand and sympathize with what they're sharing.
5. Respect your partner's point of view. This entails being on their side, even though you believe that a portion of their point of view is irrational. Maintain your sense of humor. If your connection is vital to you, it is probably more significant than your point of view on the subject.
6. Adopt a "we versus them" mentality. Make it clear to your spouse that the pair of you are in it together as a team. You are a partnership, and problems should not stand in your way. You both purposefully show a unified front in the face of anyone or anything that would want to split you.
7. Show compassion. This might vary based on your connection, so do what appears to be affection from your perspective. This might be as easy as placing

your arm around them or saying something kind to them.
8. Validate emotions. Let your partner know that their feelings make sense to you by telling them just that.

Research shows that emotional attraction is just as important as a physical attraction in having great sex. If you feel emotionally rejected by your partner, chances are that you won't be in the mood to make love.

Try this active listening exercise and see how it affects the level of emotional attraction you feel for each other: Acknowledge your feelings. Telling your spouse that their sentiments make logical sense to you is a good way to show them.

According to research, emotional appeal is equally as crucial as physical appeal when it comes to having incredible sex. When you feel emotionally shunned by your lover, you are unlikely to want to make love.

Do this eight-step active listening activity and observe how it improves your sort of personal connection with one another.

Chapter 8
30-Day Relationship Challenge

Do you want to put more significant effort into your marriage? Do you have problems in your marriage or want to improve your relationship with your spouse so that you may develop a better one? The best way to do this is to accomplish a 30-day marriage challenge! As we begin this chapter, let me explain why.

I understand how you feel if you're feeling distant from your spouse or like you're spending more time being mom and dad than husband and wife. Working schedules, school, extracurricular activities, domestic duties, dinner, bathtime, and bed routine leave you with little to no time to spend together as a pair. Dates are few and far between, and by the arrival of bedtime, you're too exhausted even to get out a proper good night.

The iMOM 30-Day Marriage Challenge and the All-Pro Dad 30-Day Challenge offer couples the opportunity to do something small daily that does not take up a lot of time but will assist in strengthening their relationship. Commit yourself to the challenge that will apply to you.

Marriage Challenge for Ladies

A 30-day marriage challenge, as the name implies, is focusing attention on your marriage for 30 days. You do one simple thing every day to reconnect and reignite the flame, allowing you to make your marriage your top priority for a month. The concept is that by the conclusion of the month, your marriage will be stronger and happier since you've spent enough time together. A 30-day marriage challenge consists of mini-challenges that encourage you to be more conscious about how you act in a married partnership and how you spend time around each other. It's entirely up to you whether you start the relationship challenge at the beginning of the month or halfway through it, and if you do it alone or both of you engage in the challenge.

iMom Printable 30-Day Challenge

- Day 1: Ask your spouse: "What is there that I can help you with today?"
- Day 2: Don't correct your husband at all today.
- Day 3: Today, hug your spouse three times.
- Day 4: Kiss your husband the first time you see him for the day.
- Day 5: Tell yourself: "My husband really loves us, and he is doing his best for us as a family."
- Day 6: Buy, make or bake his favorite food.
- Day 7: Write him a charming note for his lunch box in his suitcase or place it in his laptop.
- Day 8: Arrange at least one date on your schedule for the month.

- Day 9: Picture how it feels to be in your husband's shoes. Thank him for one thing today.
- Day 10: Focus on kindness today.
- Day 11: Say to him: "I'm so happy I chose to marry you."
- Day 12: Meditate about wisdom for being a wife.
- Day 13: Today, it's no sarcasm day. Refrain from saying what you want.
- Day 14: Think about the blessing it is to be a wife. Write it down.
- Day 15: List some positive points about your spouse.
- Day 16: Today, thank him for all he does for you.
- Day 17: Laugh together. What makes you think you'll be able to laugh with your hubby today? It isn't necessary to watch a comedy. Or, it might be pulling a prank on one another, cracking jokes, or texting him a hilarious video.
- Day 18: Think of a wife that you greatly admire. List her good points and consider how this can help you as a wife.
- Day 19: Avoid asking him to do any chores for the day. Allow him to take a break.
- Day 20: Patience is today's focal point. Take a deep breath and think before you speak.
- Day 21: If he makes a mistake, forgive him. Don't remind him of his mistakes and shortcomings.
- Day 22: Believe the best about your husband.
- Day 23: Treat him with respect.
- Day 24: Don't interrupt him when he talks. Give him the opportunity to finish his sentences.
- Day 25: Ask for your husband's opinion today. Listen to what he has to say and take it to heart.

- Day 26: Encourage him. You are his biggest supporter. Make sure he knows this.
- Day 27: Promote his wellness. Eat healthily today and/or exercise with him. Even cook together if you can.
- Day 28: Make sure he sees you looking at him with admiration today. It will make him feel appreciated and loved.
- Day 29: Turn off the distractions; TV, cellphones, and tablets must be off. Make time for your spouse by eliminating anything that may take your attention from him.
- Day 30: Focus on love today.

30 DAY MARRIAGE CHALLENGE

1. Ask, "What can I help you with today?"
2. Go the whole day without correcting your husband.
3. Hug your husband three times today.
4. Kiss your husband the first time you see him in the morning.
5. Tell yourself, "He really loves his family, and he is doing his best for us."
6. Bake, make, or buy his favorite food.
7. Leave him a sweet note.
8. Put at least one date night on your calendar this month.
9. Imagine how it feels to be in your husband's shoes.
10. Today's focus: kindness.
11. Tell him, "I'm so glad I married you."
12. Pray for wisdom in being a wife.
13. Do not use sarcasm with your husband today.
14. Remember that being a wife is a blessing.
15. Think only positive thoughts about your husband.
16. Thank him for all he does for your family.
17. Laugh with your husband today.
18. Who is a wife you admire? Try to be more like her today.
19. Don't ask him to do any chores or honey-dos.
20. Today's focus: patience.
21. Forgive him when he makes a mistake.
22. Assume the best about your husband.
23. Treat him with respect today.
24. Do not interrupt your husband when he's talking.
25. Ask your husband's opinion on something.
26. Encourage your husband.
27. Do something for his health—eat better and exercise together.
28. Look at him admiringly. Make sure he sees you looking at him.
29. Turn off the electronics—phone, TV, tablet, etc.
30. Today's focus: love.

To print your own free copy, visit the iMom website. Let's work through the requirements of the challenge.

Marriage Challenge for Men

I believe this 30-day marriage challenge will lead to significant improvements in your marriage. Simply do the specified work for that day. Your wife will like it, and your relationship may very possibly be reinvigorated by the completion of the 30 days!

- Day 1: Tell her that she looks stunning.
- Day 2: Tell her why you value her.
- Day 3: Ask her what you may help her with today.
- Day 4: Don't correct her today.
- Day 5: Today, hug her three times.
- Day 6: Kiss your wife the first time you see her today.
- Day 7: Buy her a card, write her a special note, and mail it to your house address or put it in the post box.
- Day 8: Buy her chocolate, or make her favorite dessert.
- Day 9: Book at least one date night on your schedule this month.
- Day 10: Send her a kind message.
- Day 11: Say "I'm so delighted I married you" to her.
- Day 12: In front of your children, compliment her.
- Day 13: Discuss ways in which you can do things to work for both of you.
- Day 14: Thank her for everything she does for you and your family.
- Day 15: Purchase a gift card for her favorite restaurant and set it on her dashboard.
- Day 16: When your wife is speaking, do not interrupt her. Listen to her.
- Day 17: Inquire about something with your wife.
- Day 18: Dance to your wedding song in the living room.

- Day 19: Look at her with admiration. Make sure she notices you staring at her.
- Day 20: With her, watch her favorite romantic film. There must be no mockery.
- Day 21: When your wife enters the room, turn off your phone, computer, and television.
- Day 22: Tonight, go through your wedding album.
- Day 23: Participate in an outdoor activity as a group.
- Day 24: This year, plan a romantic trip with your partner.
- Day 25: Bring her favorite dessert home with you.
- Day 26: Give her a night off from all of her responsibilities.
- Day 27: She gets a foot and neck massage.
- Day 28: Tonight, spend some extra time chatting about your thoughts.
- Day 29: "Where do you see us in 15 years?" you could ask her.
- Day 30: "I adore you because: _____"

Source: All Pro Dad.

Chapter 9
What's Cooking, Dear?

Date Night Stay-In Recipes and Ideas

Two's a Meal; Three's a Crowd

Having your date at home does not have to be boring. It can be more romantic and result in a stronger connection than a night out. Staying at home has numerous advantages, such as the ability to cook a delicious meal as a couple and eliminate the obligation of appointing a chauffeur. However, make sure that your kids are taken care of and that parents and friends don't disturb you.

At-Home Dating

Cooking together can feel like dancing together once you've found your groove in the kitchen. You each move to the rhythm of the recipe, chopping or mixing in your own space, focused while also considering your partner's tasks. As a result, there is a culinary masterpiece and a different dimension of communication, fun, and cooperation.

Let's Stay Here, Dear

True confession: I used to despise cooking. It completely intimidated me, and the mere idea of preparing a meal more complex than a green salad or a frozen ready-made dinner drove me into a state of panic and anxiety. Takeout was required for date nights in.

Perhaps you're in a similar situation: Learning to cook your own meals or running out of budget wiggle room. When you sit down to eat, you will be celebrating not only your relationship but also your progress toward a mutual objective!

If this happens to you, it is time to realize that you need to evolve out of this and start venturing out and practicing the cooking of different meals. Date nights in and cooking became especially important when we were new parents on a tight budget.

Perhaps you're moving to a new town with unfamiliar restaurants, you have a baby too small to leave at grandma's, or you've recently become empty nesters. Whatever your circumstances, having date nights at home is possible and enjoyable. All you really need are your existing dishes and appliances, as well as a trip to the grocery store and some pre-trip planning.

Savings

One of the most obvious advantages of a date night at home is the ability to save time and money. You'll have to go grocery shopping, but consider the time it takes to drive to a restaurant, wait for a table, eat, wait to pay, and then drive home. When you stay in for the night, you will almost certainly save time. You can use the extra time to reconnect with each other through an activity or an uninterrupted conversation.

How much more money would you save by cooking your own meals? When compared to a dinner at your favorite restaurant, it's quite a bit! Transportation costs (or paying a babysitter, in case you have children) will not be considered, saving you even more time and money.

You can save the money you would have spent on a night out and put it towards a vacation or other large purchase instead.

Comfort

I'm sure we're not the only ones who have a dater's block on almost every occasion we take a break. We consider not only the food but also the ambiance, service, what's available, and how crowded the restaurant is likely to be. There are so many moving parts to making a date night out work that it can become exhausting (the opposite of what you want).

It's more convenient to create your own menu, go grocery shopping, and cook together. It's not crowded at home, the atmosphere can be whatever you want it to be, and you can even change into pajamas before dinner if you wish.

Personalization and Creativity

You can also perfect your menu when you have a date night at home. You won't have to worry about allergies or requesting that your dish be prepared in a specific way. If you despise mushrooms (guilty!), you won't have to worry about them appearing in your meal. Do you think a particular herb or spice would go well in a recipe? Include it! Experimenting with different flavors in the kitchen can be a lot of fun. Make it a date.

Do you want to add a more complex dish to your menu than you usually make at home? Many people take culinary lessons to enhance their abilities and watch food shows or movies. You can take online cooking classes or watch a show or a YouTube video as you work.

If you really want to impress each other, plan your menu ahead of time and watch cooking videos to learn new skills. You can learn from each other instead of learning everything online the night of the date (It's just fun to show off!).

Ease on the Burden of Your Schedule

You can go from dinner to bed in a matter of minutes, allowing you to spend more time together without having to coordinate your schedule with a designated driver, public transportation, or a babysitter. You can even stay up until the sun comes up if you want!

While We're on the Subject of...

You're only a few steps away from your bedroom, so if you really want to go to bed early...

Make It a Game Night Too

You'll get a game, activity, or question(s) with each menu to keep the conversation going. You'll learn new things about each other, express your love in novel and creative ways, and have a good time without distractions.

Household Activities

Don't be concerned; you won't require much for the activities and games. Most of the time, you'll be fine with just a piece of paper and a pen—or no supplies at all. You can do the activities at home or wherever you are staying.

Questions in Your Conversation

The questions in the following chapters are intended to be thought-provoking, silly, fun, and nostalgic. Don't just respond and then stop talking; instead, allow the conversation to flow from there. It's even more entertaining when you disagree ("What do you mean, you'd prefer to live in New York rather than Paris?").

Invent Your Own Unique Ideas

If you come across an activity you don't want to do, a question you don't want to ask, or a rare activity that requires materials you don't have, just use what's listed as inspiration and move on. You can always substitute the activity with:

Truth, Dare, Command

Ask each other fun truth or dare questions. Toss a coin to decide who will start asking first. If you choose the truth option, you must honestly answer your spouse's question. Ask silly and fun questions. Dares can include things like foot massages or doing something strange. If you or your spouse are not willing to perform the action or answer the question, you will need to decide on a consequence like downing a shot of an alcoholic or nonalcoholic drink.

Discovering Your Love Language

Playing "Would You Rather," a game in which each player asks three questions: One silly, one normal, and one difficult/real. For example, "Would you rather be itchy all the time or have goosebumps all the time?", "Would you prefer a beach vacation or a city vacation?" and "Would you rather have no children or six children?"

A Couple of Cooks in This Kitchen

So it's date night, and you've decided to stay in and cook something tasty... together. If you're used to cooking alone, the thought of having another person in the kitchen with you may make you nervous. But don't worry, it'll be a lot of fun!

Setting up workstations and assigning tasks may not sound like a romantic evening. Still, it will have you working together in a well-choreographed dance and ensuring that everything runs smoothly.

If your kitchen has a work triangle—a layout that makes cooking easier—decide who will do the washing (of produce and possibly dishes, if you're cleaning and cooking at the same time), who will stand at the stove, and where the best place to chop vegetables and open cans are. This will assist you in staying out of each other's way.

Although the refrigerator is a part of the work triangle, ensure you have everything you need for the recipe out and at the appropriate workstations first. If you don't have a work triangle, or if your kitchen is small or galley-style, mise en place (having all of the ingredients ready before you start) is critical.

Don't forget to bring the spices, measuring cups and spoons, and any other tools you may require. I keep liquid measuring cups in the spice cabinet and measuring spoons and dry measuring cups in the drawers below. It makes it easier for me to grab everything on my mental list and move to another kitchen area if necessary.

In a confined space, flirtatiously announce your presence, so you don't run into each other until you want to. You could say "Behind you," but why not make it more fun by saying "Nice buns" or "Dancing cheek to cheek"? Discuss these phrases before you begin so that there is no confusion while the other person tries to figure out what you mean.

You'll need some fun to make this a date rather than a chore and to keep both of you entertained while you wait for the water to boil, cheese to brown, butter to melt, and so on.

If the recipe is simple, or if the job becomes a one-person job after the initial flurry of activity, one person can be designated as a chef, while the other is a bartender or DJ. Of course, the chef is in charge, but the bartender must keep the drinks topped off, and the DJ must keep the playlist fresh.

Before you begin, put on music that speaks to your soul and makes it nearly impossible not to dance together. You don't have to slow dance if that's not your style, but you should be aware of your surroundings. Don't get too excited and spill a pot of boiling water or ketchup.

Purchase the most outrageous aprons you can obtain, or simply purchase one and roll a dice to see who wears this (and maybe also have their photo posted on social media for losing the couple's bet).

It will be time to challenge yourselves after you have had plenty of practice working together in the kitchen and have your routines down. Choose a cookbook from a cuisine you're not familiar with and save some recipes to try. Try making sushi at home, preparing a vegetable you've never made before, or making the perfect macarons in an unusual flavor.

Date Night Shopping and Planning

Fear not if the shop is out of an item (I used to be concerned about this!). Simply look for a substitute or leave it out if it's a small amount, such as a teaspoon of dried oregano. I guarantee that even if you improvise a little, the recipes will still taste delicious.

Shopping for two is not the same as shopping for a larger family. If you're only buying enough to feed two people, you might want to splurge on unusual-for-you ingredients for date nights (like a more expensive cut of meat). If you regularly cook for youngsters, mix the finer foods with those they dislike, like spices or exotic veggies.

For some recipes, you might even decide to splurge on some ingredients that you wouldn't usually splurge on when shopping for regular meals. If you get the chance, try some ripe, juicy heirloom tomatoes. If you've never had one, you'll be surprised at how much more flavor they have than the regular tomatoes that most people buy when they go grocery shopping. Before a date night, my husband and I went to a farmers' market and discovered rainbow carrots. They were new to us and especially pretty; they cooked up just like regular carrots and added a special touch to dinner.

Clearly, I'm Still Considering It!

Another option is to use smaller ingredients that pack the same flavor punch as something called for in the recipe (like a shallot instead of an onion). If you usually use dried herbs, this is an excellent time to buy fresh herbs because you'll have less to chop.

You could also take a different approach and save money instead of splurging. Use this opportunity to look for deals on two packs of meat, or if you see a good deal, buy a larger package of meat with just enough for your family, plus two servings for your date night. Repackage the meat and freeze any leftovers for a future meal for the entire family.

Make a snapshot of the recipes you'll be cooking and keep it on your phone in case you need to make modifications at the supermarket. If an ingredient is out of stock, you'll be able to choose whether to substitute something else or skip it. You can probably omit the odd teaspoon of a particular herb or substitute one leafy green for another, but having the recipe in your head or on your phone will help you make the right choice.

My hope is that this chapter will not fill your pantry or spice cabinet with oddball ingredients you'll never use or excess food you'll have to throw away. The meals are for two people; however, portions may be left over for the following day based on appetite. If you find a recipe you want to share, feel free to multiply the ingredients and substitute more affordable (or larger) options, such as onions instead of shallots or regular tomatoes instead of heirloom tomatoes.

The recipes use common ingredients that are prepared in a unique way so that you can use the leftovers later. In certain circumstances, you may thaw extra (like meat bought at a discount) and utilize it again the following evening, cutting costs.

What You Will Find in This Chapter

Are you ready to start this date? Here's what you can expect.

From the "romantic Anniversary steakhouse dinner" to the more casual "chatting over comfort food and Thursday game night date," these menus are all themed. With 20 menus featuring a wide range of date night favorites, there is something for everyone.

It's simple to wind up in a traditional school group scenario, as with any activity which involves more than one participant. You know what I mean: When all are trying to do their unique stuff (or only watching) and hoping that everything will magically fall into place at the end. Enter the role of the sous-chef to avoid this unfavorable outcome! A sous-chef is essentially an assistant chef who assists in the preparation of ingredients and fills in wherever needed. Sometimes that entails pouring a glass of wine for their partner after all the vegetables have been chopped and tossed into the pot!

You'll notice that almost all of the recipes include instructions. As you work your way through the recipes, make sure everyone gets a turn as a chef and a turn as a sous-chef. Thus, one spouse is in charge, and the other assists, making turns for each dish or date. If you come across a recipe for your favorite dish, you may decide to take the initiative. Your partner, on the other hand, may want to do the majority of the work and treat you to a lovely dinner featuring the foods you enjoy the most. Some recipes are simply more manageable for one person to prepare, and that's perfectly fine. The sous-chef will still have tasks to complete.

Is this your first time having a date night at home? Taco Tuesday is a deceptively simple dish. It appears to be a lot of work at the start, but it's a whole lot of fun and an easy introduction to date night cooking.

Labels on the recipes will help you narrow down your options based on how much time you have, what you're in the mood for, how much attention you want to give the cooking portion of your evening, and what you might have on hand. Basic ingredient recipes consist of five ingredients (excluding basics like oil and sugar). More time-consuming recipes are those that can be prepared and completed in half an hour maximum.

To make things easier, try to use one pot or pan for recipes that can be entirely prepared in a single pot or pan, to save on doing the dishes afterwards or the next day. Or, if you are not bothered with elegance, serve your food in take-out containers or paper plates, and avoid the dishes entirely!

Vegetarian/vegan dishes refer to recipes that use few or no animal products.

If an ingredient is missing, out of stock, or whatever the case may be, Google for possible substitutes or discuss alternatives that can work with your spouse.

Activities

You'll find a game, activity, prompt, or question to take your date to the next level with each menu, but feel free to choose one from another menu, add your own, or use the recommendation as a jumping-off point to create an entirely new activity or to spark conversation. Make it sexier, personalize it for your relationship and personalities, or even put money on the line.

Recipe for a Full English Breakfast for Two People

Ingredients

- 4 pork sausages
- 4 slices of back bacon
- Mushrooms, sliced (about 6 ounces)
- 1 cup canned beans with tomato sauce
- 2 ripe tomatoes, cut in half
- A pinch of salt
- 2 slices of black pudding
- 2 slices of white bread
- 4 large eggs

Cooking Instructions

1. Preheat the oven to 200 degrees Fahrenheit.
2. Place an ovenproof dish in the oven to keep it warm while you're cooking.
3. Using a large frying pan, heat the vegetable oil over medium heat until it shimmers.
4. Cook the sausages in the pan for approximately 10 minutes or until they are browned on both sides.
5. While the sausages are cooking, add the bacon to the pan and heat until the bacon is crispy.
6. Heat the bacon for 3-5 minutes on each side, and then add the mushrooms and cook until the mushrooms are browned.
7. When the sausages, bacon, and mushrooms are finished cooking, move them to an ovenproof dish,

cover them with foil, and place them in the oven to keep warm while you prepare the other ingredients.
8. Add the beans to a small saucepan and simmer over medium-low heat, stirring occasionally.
9. Remove the frying pan from the heat and coat it with vegetable oil.
10. Test and season the tomatoes with salt before adding them to the pan, flesh side down.
11. Add the black pudding to the same pan and heat for 2 minutes on each side until the black pudding is cooked through.
12. Remove it from the oven and transfer it to a baking dish.
13. Remove the pan from the heat and add 3 tablespoons of vegetable oil, heating over medium-high heat until the oil is hot. Cook the bread in the oil until it is golden brown (try it by dropping a corner of bread into the oil; if it sizzles, it is ready).
14. Remove the foil from the sausages, bacon, and mushrooms. Allow the excess liquid to drain.
15. Add the eggs to the same oil and fry the yolks by spooning heated oil over them until they are done.
16. Place all of the components on a dish and serve the bread on the side as a garnish.

Breakfast in Bed

It is not necessary to battle weekend crowds if you like to have brunch in your love nest instead. To be honest, you won't even have to get out of your PJs. Create a romantic atmosphere by serving your lover chocolate waffles or heart-shaped pancakes in bed on a leisurely Saturday or Sunday. It's hard to imagine anything better than chocolates for your sweetie. And if you think that this recipe for chocolate waffles isn't rich enough, read on for a recipe for red velvet doughnuts instead.

Chocolate Waffles - A Delicious Treat

Chocolate waffles are a decadent delicacy that can be enjoyed at any time of the day or night.

- Preparation time: 25 minutes
- Makes a total of 8 delicious waffles

Ingredients

- 1 packet Classic Dark Chocolate Fudge Cake Mix
- 1 cup of distilled water
- 3 free-range eggs
- ½ cup extra-virgin olive oil
- Cooking spray with a non-stick coating
- 1 cup fresh strawberries, finely diced
- Chocolate syrup
- Whipped cream, to be used as a finishing touch

Cooking Instructions

1. In a large mixing bowl, combine the cake mix, water, oil, and eggs at a moderate pace with your electric hand mixer until moistened (about 30 seconds). Mix for a further 2 minutes at medium speed.
2. Spray the cooking spray on the grids of a waffle iron and warm the iron according to the manufacturer's instructions.
3. Pour the batter into the waffle iron and cook it according to the manufacturer's instructions.

4. Remove the waffle from the iron and serve it immediately or keep it warm until serving time. Strawberries, chocolate syrup, and whipped cream may be added as garnishes if desired (Ready Set Eat Chocolate Cake Waffles).

Pancakes in the Form of Chocolate Hearts

Warm, heart-shaped pancakes cooked with hot cocoa mix and pancake mix, drizzled with a simple marshmallow sauce, and topped with whipped cream for a festive treat.

- Preparation time: 30 minutes
- Makes 6 servings.

Ingredients

- Non-stick cooking spray
- 2 cups pancake mix
- 3 x (1.38 oz) Swiss Miss® Milk Chocolate Hot Cocoa Mix
- 1-½ cups low-fat (2%) milk
- 2 eggs
- 3 cups mini marshmallows
- 1 tablespoon margarine
- Whipped cream

Instructions

1. Spray two 5-inch heart-shaped metal cookie cutters with cooking spray and a large pan or skillet with cooking spray. Heat a skillet over medium heat until it is hot to the touch.

2. Meanwhile, whisk together the pancake mix, cocoa mix, milk, and eggs in a medium-sized mixing basin until well combined. Cutters should be placed in a skillet. Distribute a ¼ cup of batter into each cutter, spreading the batter to the edges of each cutter—Cook for 2 to 3 minutes, or until bubbles appear on the surface. Using caution, carefully remove the cutters; flip the pan and cook until the other side is done. Make a second batch with the leftover batter, spritzing cutters with cooking spray as necessary. Maintain the temperature of the pancakes.
3. Using a medium microwave-safe dish, combine the marshmallows and margarine; microwave on HIGH for 45 seconds, or until the marshmallows are melted, and the mixture is well blended when the bowl is swirled. 3 seconds later, stir in whipped cream (about 1 cup). 1 tablespoon of sauce and a dish of whipped cream should be put on top of every pancake.

Hint: If you can't find 5-inch heart-shaped cookie cutters, use smaller cutters with less batter or simply make ordinary pancakes without the shapes if they're not available.

A pre-mixed, multi-purpose baking mix comprising ingredients such as sugar, salt, butter or oil, and baking powder agents is referred to as an "original baking mix." You may make your own at home using ordinary pantry goods, or you can buy them in the baking department of your local supermarket if you choose convenience over quality (Ready, Set, Eat Chocolate Heart-Shaped Pancakes).

Red Velvet Donuts

Red velvet donuts are a delightful morning treat that is both delicious and simple to create.

- Preparation time: 20 minutes
- Total time: 40 minutes
- Makes 20 doughnuts

Ingredients

- Non-stick cooking spray
- 1 package (15.25 oz) Red Velvet Cake Mix
- 2 eggs
- ½ cup of melted butter
- 1 cup of full cream milk
- 1 cup vanilla or chocolate creamy frosting
- Sprinkles

Instructions

1. Preheat the oven to 350 degrees Fahrenheit. Cooking spray should be used to coat the doughnut pan.
2. Whisk together the cake mix, eggs, butter, and milk in a large mixing basin until smooth.
3. Fill a tubing or zipped plastic bag with a corner cut off, and pipe the mixture into the bag.
4. Fill the donut pan halfway with batter (but don't completely fill it!).
5. Bake the donuts in the preheated oven. Remove donuts from the pan as soon as possible and let them cool fully on a cooling rack.

6. Warm icing in the microwave for 15 seconds to decorate. Dot the tops of the donuts with frosting and garnish with sprinkles (Ready Set Eat Red Velvet Donuts).

Bolognese Spaghetti Made with Lentils

This delicious family classic has suddenly become a whole lot nicer thanks to a new ingredient.

- Preparation time: 40 minutes
- Makes 6 servings

Ingredients

- 2 garlic cloves, peeled (optional)
- 1 small onion, peeled and sliced
- 1 medium carrot chopped
- 6 oz. mushrooms, chopped
- 1 tablespoon extra-virgin olive oil
- ½ teaspoon of dried oregano
- ¼ teaspoon crushed red pepper flakes
- Kosher salt and freshly ground pepper
- 8 ounces of lean ground beef
- 1 tablespoon of tomato paste
- Whole tomatoes from a 14-ounce can
- ½ cup of dry red lentils
- 1 pound of spaghetti
- ⅓ cup of roasted pine nuts (optional)
- Pecorino cheese, grated, to be used as a garnish (optional)

Instructions

1. In a food processor, blitz the onion, garlic, mushrooms, and carrot, until they are thoroughly minced and combined, about 30 seconds.
2. On medium heat, heat the oil in a big pan. Cook covered, turning frequently, for 4 to 5 minutes, or until veggies are soft. Season with oregano and red pepper flakes, ¼ teaspoon each salt and pepper, and ¼ teaspoon each garlic powder and onion powder. Simmer for 10 to 12 minutes, splitting up the steak with a spoon, until the beef is brown.
3. Simmer for 1 minute after adding the tomato paste. Add tomatoes (including their juices) to the pan, smashing them with your fingers as you add them. Cook for 15 to 20 minutes, occasionally stirring, until lentils are cooked. Add 2 cups of water and ¼ teaspoon salt and pepper.
4. In the meantime, prepare the pasta according to package guidelines. Drain the pasta and combine it with the sauce. Garnish with pine nuts and cheese (The Good Housekeeping Test Kitchen) if you like.

Activity: Create the Feeling

When you're having a date night staying in, you really shouldn't scrimp on the ambiance. A new tablecloth, swirling candle lights, quiet music that suits the mood, and fine dishes and silverware elevate the occasion from pleasant to extraordinary. So why should we halt here at all? Make an effort to be inventive and innovative in your approach. Imagine you're the restaurant manager trying to set the atmosphere so that your customers can not wait to come back. You may also eat outside on the terrace or in a different room. In the lounge room, sit on a quilt or utilize the cocktail table while sitting on cushions. Put flowers or greenery from the garden (they wouldn't have to be roses, anything attractive and lush!) in a vase.

Despite the fact that you realize you won't utilize them, it is more about how you promote yourself! Get ready for supper, whether that entails nice clothing and a coordinating pair of PJs, and slip a voucher for dishwashing duty beneath the linen napkin (Schwanke).

Salad Wraps With Hot Shrimp

The key ingredient in the shrimp salad wraps is gochujang (Korean red pepper paste sauce) (MacAvoy and Merker).

- Preparation time: 25 minutes
- Makes 6 servings

Set a plate of nutritious shrimp salad wraps cooked with vegetables and herbs for your date. In order to keep the spiciness at bay, the shrimp are flavored with gochujang, fresh ginger, and garlic before being wrapped in a cold, crisp Boston lettuce cup. With a prep. time of below 30 minutes, it is the ideal simple supper dish or healthy lunch option that can be served hot or cold.

A jar of gochujang can enhance the taste of any food you prepare. It's a pickled paste from gochugaru, a Korean red pepper, and a combination of flours and other ingredients. The sauces in this recipe benefit from the addition of a fiery bite, as well as a moderate sweetness. Quick hint: Since each jar will have a distinct amount of spice, it's important to taste a tiny bit before putting it in your food to ensure that you don't mistakenly go overboard with the heat.

Grilling shrimp in the oven is a hands-off approach that creates less mess than searing them in a skillet, and it's fast and straightforward. The tastes of the sweet, spicy, delightful marinade are concentrated and developed as a result of this process. As an added bonus, it makes it simple to increase the shrimp dish to serve as leftovers the following day by simply baking another sheet pan in the oven.

Take note that Boston lettuce is also known as butter lettuce or Bibb lettuce when shopping for it, and either of these varieties will work in this dish. If you are unable to locate them, Romaine lettuce makes an excellent replacement. Simply tear apart the lettuce to create little "boats" that are great for filling with shrimp.

Ingredients

- 2 tablespoons freshly squeezed lemon juice
- 1 to 2 tablespoons of gochujang (Korean hot pepper paste)
- 1 tablespoon extra-virgin olive oil
- 2 teaspoons of honey
- 1 garlic clove, minced
- 2 teaspoons ginger, freshly grated
- 1 ½ pounds shrimp, peeled and deveined
- 1 head of Boston lettuce, leaves removed
- 1 bunch of Persian cucumbers, thinly sliced
- Small radishes, sliced
- Sliced mint and basil, which will be used for serving

Instructions

Preheat the oven to 425 degrees Fahrenheit. A big mixing basin is ideal for mixing lemon juice, gochujang, oil, and honey together before adding the garlic and ginger. Toss in the shrimp to coat them in the sauce.

Place the vegetables in a single layer on a rimmed baking sheet and roast for 10 to 15 minutes until they are barely opaque.

Serve the shrimp on a bed of lettuce with cucumbers, radishes, mint, and basil on top.

What Activity Would You Choose?

Get to know your partner better by creating serious and ludicrous circumstances in which you must choose between two options. Because this type of game is frequently used as an icebreaker at small parties, you may have played something similar previously. Make a list of questions ahead of schedule or allow them to flow to you naturally. Time to complete: 15 - 30 minutes.

Instructions

Do it individually, selecting one of two options for each other. It might be whatever, from general tastes to bizarre circumstances you'd seldom encounter. Here are some examples to get you going: Do you prefer the morning or the evening? Humming every moment, words are coming from your lips or leaping and dancing everywhere you go (rather than strolling)? To be unable to wear slippers or eat your favorite meals once more? Is it better to get a massage or to cuddle? To have a lizard connected to your wrist for a week or go a month without using your phone? Don't hesitate to ask your partner about their decision-making approach as they respond in order to obtain insight into how their brain operates. Continue to take rounds as long as you prefer to!

Linguine with Roasted Ratatouille

These fresh veggies are pretty stunning—and you'll be surprised to learn that you can dress up a plate of your favorite noodles in just 25 minutes.

Why limit yourself to just one summer vegetable when you can have five?

- Preparation time: 25 minutes
- Makes 4 servings

Ingredients

- 12 ounces of linguine
- 2 cups small zucchini, sliced lengthwise
- 1 small eggplant, cut lengthwise across the middle
- 1 red pepper, halved
- 1 yellow pepper, halved
- 1 red onion, cut into rounds
- 2 tablespoons extra-virgin olive oil
- Freshly grated parmesan cheese and chopped basil for garnish, if desired

Instructions

1. Preheat the cooker to medium-high heat. Cook the linguine according to the package guidelines. Prep the vegetables by brushing them with oil and seasoning with ½ a teaspoon each of salt and pepper. In the meantime, prepare the vegetables.

2. Grill veggies for 3 to 4 minutes on each side, or until they are barely soft. Then transfer the mixture to a cutting board and cut it into slices.

Toss the linguine with the grilled veggies, adding more olive oil if necessary. Finish with a sprinkling of grated cheese and herbs of your choice. With a caloric intake of less than 500, this is a spaghetti dish you can eat without stress.

Exercise: Making Word Connections

Playing this game as you cook is a blast because it's quick and easy to pick up and put down (Schwanke). In the future, you may find yourself playing the game while taking a stroll, driving, or even doing housework or relaxing on the sofa with your partner.

Provisions required: Set the stopwatch (borrow a time glass from an old board game or set the stopwatch on your phone)

Time required: As much or as little as you choose to devote to it.

Guidelines: Set a one-minute timer.

One individual utters a unique phrase. You then must tell your spouse to express whatever jumps to mind without filtering. As soon as a word comes to mind for the first player, they say it aloud. Continue moving back and forth until the clock runs out. Who knows? You could find yourself telling stories among sentences just for a laugh ("What? When I asked, 'How did you come to that term from that?'"). If you'd rather not have a timer, you may just carry on playing! The following is an example: The first spouse says "Coffee," and the second spouse jumps to answer "Cup." The first spouse responds with

"Cupcake," and the second says "Happy Birthday!" Make the game even more difficult by introducing a restriction. There are a number of examples, such as all words starting with the same character, the same categories, rhyming, etcetera.

Chicken with Carrots and Couscous in a Hot Sesame Sauce

Sweet and salty in equal measure, this dish is just bursting with taste.

- Prep. time: 10 minutes
- Total time: 40 minutes
- Makes 4 servings

Ingredients

- 1 tablespoon coriander seeds, finely chopped
- 1 tablespoon sesame seeds
- 1 teaspoon cumin seeds, finely ground
- ½ teaspoon peppercorns, finely ground
- 6 small to medium carrots, split lengthwise and chopped into 2-inch chunks.
- 2 tablespoons extra-virgin olive oil
- Kosher salt
- 4 tiny chicken legs, split (4 thighs, 4 drumsticks)
- 1¼ cup cooked couscous
- 1 teaspoon finely grated lime zest combined with 2 tablespoons lime juice
- 2 thinly sliced scallions
- 12 cup cilantro, finely chopped

Instructions

1. Preheat the oven to 450 degrees Fahrenheit. Combine the coriander seeds, sesame seeds, cumin seeds, and pepper in a small bowl.
2. On a large rimmed baking sheet, mix the carrots with 1 tablespoon oil and ¼ teaspoon salt until evenly coated. After rubbing the chicken with ½ tablespoon oil and seasoning with ½ teaspoon salt, coat it with the spice blend. Place the chicken on the same baking sheet with the skin side down and roast until the chicken is cooked through and the carrots are golden brown and soft about 28 to 30 minutes.
3. In the meanwhile, prepare the couscous according to package guidelines. Fluff with a fork, then mix with lime juice and the remaining ½ tablespoon oil before folding in the scallions, cilantro, and lime zest to finish. Serve with chicken and carrots as a side dish.

Cauli-Steaks

These cauliflower "steaks" with Chimichurri sauce are a delicious vegetarian dish. Cauliflower steaks may be prepared in about 20 minutes. They're a fast and straightforward vegetarian option that anybody can make.

If you say the term "steak" to most people, a large slab of cauliflower isn't the first thing that springs to mind. This delicious cauliflower steak dish, created by the Good Housekeeping Test Kitchen experts, will change all of that. It's a meatless supper option that even the most devoted meat lovers will like.

The greatest thing about these steaks is that they can be prepared in just 20 minutes, making them ideal for serving as a fast and simple midweek supper. Simply follow these suggestions from our pros and get to work:

Cauliflower should be cut with care. The cauliflower must preserve its form if you want to finish up with a proper cauliflower "steak." To understand what we mean, have a look at the video above.

Look for creative methods to make use of the remaining cauliflower. To create your own cauliflower rice, pulse the leftover pieces in a food processor until finely chopped, or slice them into bite-size florets to grill.

Bring your imagination to bear. This easy recipe provides many options to experiment with different flavors: You may use any combination of herbs and spices to season your cauliflower, such as black pepper, curry powder, rosemary, or lemon zest, to flavor it. Tzatziki, pesto, chutney, or creamy horseradish would all be delicious accompaniments to your ribs, and you can mix up the sauce based on your seasoning.

- Preparation time: 5 minutes
- Total time: 20 minutes
- Makes 2 servings

Ingredients

- 1 large head of cauliflower
- 1 teaspoon cumin seeds, ground
- 5 tablespoons of canola oil
- ¼ cup finely chopped cilantro packed loosely in a small bowl

- ¼ cup finely chopped fresh parsley leaves packed loosely together
- 3 tablespoons of red wine vinegar
- 1 tiny clove of garlic, pounded with a press
- The seeds and coarsely diced flesh of 1 jalapeno chili
- ¼ teaspoon salt is sprinkled on top.

Instructions

1. Cauliflower should have its leaves and any extra stem removed. Place the cauliflower on its stem end and chop off about 14 inches of the stem end. Using a sharp knife, cut 2 slices from the middle of the cauliflower (each approximately 1 inch thick); save the rounded wedges for later use.
2. Combine cumin and 1 tablespoon of canola oil in a small bowl. Using a pastry brush, coat all of the cauliflower pieces.
3. Heat 2 tablespoons of oil in a 12-inch oven-safe skillet over medium-high heat until heated.
4. Cook for 3 minutes after adding the cauliflower. Slices should be turned over.
5. Place the pan in a 425-degree Fahrenheit oven and roast for 15 to 20 minutes, or until the stem is soft when poked with the tip of a paring knife, depending on how big your skillet is.
6. In the meanwhile, combine the cilantro, parsley, vinegar, garlic, jalapeno, remaining 2 tbsp. oil, and 18 tsp. salt in a large mixing bowl. Finish by spooning herb sauce over the cooked "steaks."

Lamb Chops With a Salad of Peas

Served with luscious roasted lamb chops, a fresh and crisp salad of mildly pickled fennel and onion, snap peas, and herbs will enliven the dish.

- Preparation time: 35 minutes
- Makes 4 servings

Ingredients

For lamb chops, combine:

- ½ red onion, finely diced
- 2 tablespoons rice vinegar
- Kosher salt and pepper to taste
- 1 rack of lamb that has been trimmed
- 2 ½ tablespoon olive oil—divided
- 2 ½ teaspoon coriander—crushed
- 1 ½ teaspoon ground sumac—prepared as directed on the package
- ¼ cup finely chopped fresh mint
- 2 tablespoons finely chopped flat-leaf parsley

If You're Making Salad

- 1 ½ tablespoons freshly squeezed lemon juice
- 1 tablespoon extra-virgin olive oil
- A pinch of salt
- A pinch of sugar
- Kosher salt and pepper to taste
- 1 small fennel bulb, thinly sliced
- ¼ red onion, finely sliced (this is important)
- 6 cups sugar snap peas, peeled and halved lengthwise

- ¼ cup flat-leaf parsley leaves (optional)
- ¼ cup of tiny mint leaves
- ¼ cup of small basil leaves

Instructions

1. Preheat the oven to 425 degrees Fahrenheit. Make lamb by following these steps: Combine the onions, vinegar, and ¼ tsp salt in a small mixing dish. Allow to rest until the lamb is done.
2. Rub 1 tablespoon of oil over the meat and sprinkle with coriander, sumac, and half a teaspoon each salt and pepper. Place on a rimmed baking pan and bake until done. Roast until desired doneness is reached, about 20 to 25 minutes for medium-rare meat. Allow for at least 10 minutes of resting time before slicing.
3. Meanwhile, prepare the salad: In a medium-sized mixing bowl, whisk together the lemon juice, oil, sugar, and half a teaspoon each of salt and pepper until the sugar is completely dissolved. Allow the fennel and onion to settle for 10 minutes, stirring regularly, before folding in the snap peas and fresh herbs. Make a mental note to put it away.
4. While the lamb is resting, whisk in the remaining tablespoon of oil to the onion mixture, followed by the mint and parsley, and toss well.

Serving suggestions: Cut meat into chops and serve with a salad dressed with onion and herb dressing.

After Dinner Date Activity: Thank You for Your Kind Words From All Around the World

When we appreciate something about our spouse, it's easy to forget to express our feelings verbally. Take a minute to compliment one another on their wonderful characteristics—this time in a foreign language. Nothing is off-limits in this world. Time to properly look at each other or to express what you've been thinking all along is essential.

The following materials are required:

- Internet access and/or
- The use of a translation application

Time frame: 5 to 10 minutes is anticipated

Instructions

Start by looking for a website or mobile application that will enable you to translate sentences from one language to another. You may choose any language. Consider anything you'd want to commend your spouse on, then put it into the translator's text box. You may read it aloud or listen to it on the website or app.

Leave it up to your spouse to guess which praise you're referring to.

Change places with your spouse, accept a compliment from them and attempt to figure out what they said. Who received the compliment that was the most original or thoughtful? Experiment with amusing and surprising compliments, and swap out the languages as much as you'd want to keep things interesting. You'll both feel lighter, better, and more valued after participating in the exercise.

Work on this weekly, every day, or every evening, and incorporate it into your normal activities.

Write down your best compliments and the words you used to say them on the following lines as a reminder of the things you like in one another's personalities.

_____

_____

_____

_____

_____

_____

_____

_____

I'm Lookin' for a Pizza Your Heart

Make a pizza according to your heart's whim (Excel, n.d). I'm sure you're a fan of pizza since, well, who isn't? You may not realize this, but you have a real passion for making pizza! Get creative by sprinkling your favorite ingredients over a homemade base. Alternatively, you may each create a pizza and compete against each other in a pizza-making competition. If you're looking for a fun double date or a one-on-one, here's the delicious competition for you!

The Pizza Dough

You can add any herbs or spices that you think will taste good.

Preparation time: 32 minutes

Ingredients:

- 4 cups of bread flour (can substitute all-purpose flour, but bread flour makes a crispier pizza base)
- 1 tablespoon of sugar
- 1 packet of dry yeast
- A pinch of salt
- 1 ½ cups warm water (around 110 degrees fahrenheit)
- 2 tbsp. olive oil
- 2 tbsp. cumin seeds

Instructions:

1. Combine flour, sugar, yeast, and salt in a stand mixer.
2. Add the water and 2 tablespoons of oil to the mixer and mix until a pastry ball develops. The dough should come together into a firm ball with the addition of extra flour, one tbsp until it is no longer gooey. Add additional water, 1 tbsp at a time, if the batter is too dry.
3. Using a lightly floured surface, gradually knead the dough into a smooth and firm ball. A big bowl should be sprayed with the remaining teaspoons of olive oil, and the dough should be placed inside, covered with plastic wrap, in a warm area for approximately an hour to rise.
4. Once risen, divide the dough in half and roll it out to a thin layer on a lightly floured board. Allow them to rest for ten minutes after covering with a kitchen towel or plastic wrap. Sauce and toppings on, bake for 8-10 minutes at 450 degrees Fahrenheit.

The Pizza Sauce

- Can of undrained, diced tomatoes
- Can of tomato paste
- 1 tablespoon of sugar
- ¼ teaspoon of oregano powder
- ¼ teaspoon garlic salt
- 1 dried basil leaf, minced
- ¼ teaspoon red pepper flakes

Instructions

Blend or process all ingredients until desired consistency is achieved in a blender or food processor. Adjust the seasonings according to your preference.

These are some of the recipes we found on the web, adapted from various sources: https://www.melskitchencafe.com/homemade-pizza-sauce/ www.foodnetwork.com/recipes/bobby-flay/pizza-dough-recipe-1921714

Dark Chocolate Mousse With Fresh Raspberries

If you're looking for a delicious date dessert, this is it!

Easy is the rating.

Preparation time: 30 minutes

Notes: It is recommended that you prepare this delicacy earlier in the day or the day before to allow it to firm up. You can still do it together, though. See it as preparations for your date.

Ingredients:

- 16 oz dark (cocoa) chocolate with a hint of sweetness

- 1 extra-large egg
- 1 cup of cream, whipped
- 1 tablespoon of sugar
- Can of whipped cream for topping
- Approx. 8-10 berries, fresh or frozen (optional)

Instructions:

1. In a saucepan or double boiler, bring 3-4 inches of water to boil slowly, then drop the heat to medium-low or low to keep the water from boiling over.
2. Place a metal bowl that is slightly bigger than the saucepan on top of the pot of water cooking over low heat. Pour in the whipped cream and heat until it is hot but not boiling.
3. Crumble the chocolate into tiny chunks and place it in a mixing basin with the sugar. Stir regularly with a wooden spoon until the chocolate is completely melted. Whenever the chocolate has melted entirely, withdraw it from the burner and set the bowl in a bigger basin filled with cold water to cool completely.
4. The egg whites should be separated from the egg yolks and poured into a mixing bowl after the chocolate has reached room temperature. Whip the egg whites with an electric blender until they are firm and you have little peaks in the middle of them.
5. Using a light hand, gradually fold the egg white into the cooled-off chocolate until it is totally incorporated. Spoon the chocolate mousse into two separate pudding bowls to set.
6. To cool, wrap each bowl tightly in plastic wrap and place it in the fridge for a number of hours or overnight until it has cooled completely. Serve with a

dollop of whipped cream on top and a couple of raspberries or any other berry of your choice for garnish (Bunt).

Recipe for a Chocolate Shake With Red Wine

This recipe includes chocolate ice cream, red wine, and chocolate syrup. There's no need to get fancy with these tastes; they're delicious on their own. Experiment with different variations. Make it with vanilla ice cream, for instance, and see how it turns out.

Wine shakes have grown increasingly popular in recent years. Trish Bozeman's chocolate red wine milkshake recipe (Bozeman, 2020) uses only four ingredients: Chocolate ice cream, wine, chocolate syrup, and whipped cream. This is the ideal Valentine's Day treat to share with a wine-enthusiast spouse.

Today, you'll be treated to chocolate, and red wine shakes! A formalized term for a perfect dessert. To be precise, everything has been blended in a delectable, wonderful, chocolaty, winey milkshake. Oh my goodness, my friends, this is the stuff that dreams are made of.

Okay, it sounds a little out of the ordinary, doesn't it? However, wine shakes have grown increasingly popular in recent years. It is a delicious item that converts everyone into believers in the power of chocolate wine milkshakes.

It's hard to beat the combination of red wine and chocolate. In a great way, the flavors come together in this dish; so appealing.

Experiment with the following variations:

- Make it with various flavors of ice cream and see how it turns out.
- Shake it up with a shot of vodka.
- Incorporate sparkling wine into the drink!
- 100g cold butter, cut into small pieces, in a bowl
- One medium egg yolk

Items needed to make the filling: Doesn't the combination of chocolate and red wine seem a little... romantic?

Even though this wine shake recipe is quick and easy to make, it is nice enough to serve as a Valentine's day treat.

Because it is not something you want to consume in excess, this recipe only produces enough for two people. So whip up a batch soon after dinner and enjoy your dessert with a glass of wine to accompany it!

Are you not a fan of Valentine's Day? Make these for a date night staying in! You make a choice!

Bananas Fried With Brown Sugar and Cinnamon

Easy is the rating.

Preparation time: 15–20 minutes

- 2 bananas (ripe), cut into bite-size chunks
- 2 tablespoons of brown sugar
- Butter
- A can of whipped cream for topping
- Cinnamon (optional)

Instructions:

1. Melt 2-3 tablespoons of butter in a small nonstick skillet over medium heat until the butter is melted. Keep an eye on the butter to ensure it doesn't burn.
2. Once the butter has melted, place the bananas and brown sugar in the skillet, and cook until the bananas are soft. As the butter is melting away, add more.
3. Brown sugar and bananas should be heated together until the sugar has melted and covered the bananas. The bananas will still be warm (about 2-3 minutes). Place the bananas on two dessert dishes and dot the tops with whipped cream. Sprinkle with cinnamon if you prefer (Bunt).

Activity: Exchange a Compliment for a Hug

Serve your spouse with a compliment. In exchange, to show their appreciation, they should hug you. Take turns altering between compliments and sincere hugs.

"I love being married. It's so great to find that one special person you want to annoy for the rest of your life." —Rita Rudner

Picnic on the Go Recipe - Deviled Eggs

If you want to make something tasty for your picnic date, all boxes are checked with these deviled eggs.

This recipe has a lot of protein and healthy fats that you can make in no time. Vitamin B and other good nutrients are also found in this recipe. It's very easy to make your own piper bag by filling a sealable bag with your yummy egg mixture and cutting off one of the edges. Place your yellow egg halves back into the egg dish and pipe the egg yolk back into the egg white bowls. This is how you do it:

The chef (spouse A) should prepare the spice and yolks mixture for the recipe, and the sous-chef (spouse B) should pipe the mixture into the egg white cups.

Makes 6 servings

Ingredients

- 6 hard-boiled eggs (halved)
- 12 cups of mayo
- 1 tsp of mustard powder
- 1 tablespoon of condensed milk
- Salt and pepper
- 4 tablespoons of garlic powder
- Paprika
- Parsley, chopped
- Green onions, chopped

Instructions

1. When the eggs are done cooking, they should be hard-boiled.
2. Remove the hard-boiled egg yolks from the halves of the eggs. Put them in a bowl. With your fork, smash the yolks.
3. Mix all the ingredients with the yolks in a bowl, then stir in the flour.
4. When you're done, pipe the yokes into the white parts of the eggs.
5. Parsley and spring onions should be put on top.

Activity: Plan Your Picnic

This may be ideal for summer or springtime. Discuss options with your partner, or inform them that you are planning a surprise. List possible locations for your picnic and what you will need to make it a success. Remember to pack a comfy blanket to sit on and insect repellent to prevent any bugs from infecting your love story.

Other quick snack ideas for a picnic: Quiches, sandwiches, wraps, pies, and pasta salads. Remember to pack enough beverages, so you stay cool and hydrated!

The Picnic Pastry Idea (Quiche Tarts)

Preparation time: up to 90 minutes. Then, chill for another hour.

Makes 10 servings

They have a short pastry crust, cherry tomato, and cheese filling that is easy to eat on the go. They are great for picnics in the park and summer days at the beach.

Items needed to make the pastry:

- 180g flour, plus extra for sprinkling
- 400g pack of cherry tomatoes
- Olive oil, for drizzling on the food
- 90g of pancetta rashers (90g packages are very thin)
- 100g of parmesan cheese, grated
- 3 eggs, as well as 5 egg yolks
- 250ml (one cup) of double cream
- 2 small packages of basil, chopped very small

- 10 tartlet pans to make the tartlets (about 7.5cm in diameter each)

Instructions

1. Turn on the oven to 400 degrees Fahrenheit. Pour olive oil over the tomatoes and season them. Roast them for about 25-30 minutes until they start shrinking and darken. Take them out, let them cool, and then put them back in the oven.
2. Dry-fry the pancetta until it's crispy and golden brown. Leave on a plate lined with kitchen paper and cool.
3. In the meantime, make the pastry. Add the flour and ½ tsp salt to a food processor and pulse a few times. Add the butter and blitz for about 20 seconds until you have a very fine crumb. As long as the machine is running, add 2-3 tbsp of ice-cold water and 1 egg yolk. The dough should be formed, but don't over-mix. Make a lump out of the dough and wrap it in cling film. Then chill for at least 30 minutes, but no more than an hour.
4. Roll out the dough to the thickness of a lasagna sheet. You'll line each one with some pastry by cutting a circle around a plate or bowl that's a little bigger than the tartlet pans. The pastry should be pressed into a fluted edge. The excess should fall over the top edge, and you should run a rolling pin over the top of the tins to cut off the pastry. Re-roll the pastry scraps until you've lined all of your pans. Then put them back in the fridge for 30 minutes or until they're hard and ready to use again.

5. Turn on the oven to 400 degrees Fahrenheit again. For 10 minutes, bake the tarts in the oven with baking parchment and baking beans on them. Then, take out the paper and the beans. Bake for another 5 minutes, until the bread just starts to get a little brown. As soon as the cases come out of the oven, brush them with egg white all over. This makes a seal to keep the pastry from getting moist from the filling, making the pastry case more crispy.
6. In each tart case, spread half of the grated cheese and crumble the crispy pancetta on top. Nestle the roasted tomatoes in, then add the rest of the cheese on top.
7. Mix the rest of the eggs, the cream, and perhaps some black pepper in a jug. Add the basil and mix it in again. You should place a baking tray in the oven to heat. Then, put the quiche shells on the baking tray and carefully pour the egg mixture over them. Bake for about 20 to 25 minutes, until the bread is golden and puffs up a little. Cooking times for air fryer ovens may vary, so please check your device specifications. Cool down, then store in the fridge until it's ready to serve. It can be prepared up to a day before your picnic. Enjoy!

Conclusion

Oh no, you have reached the end of this book! I hope you had lots of fun with your spouse. Think about which activities you enjoyed the most, which activities taught you the most about yourself and one another, and which activities were easy to complete when the time was a delicacy. You are welcome to engage in these activities again in the future or even develop some of your own! The sky is the limit, so reach for the stars!

If you've started putting the concepts from this book into practice, you've undoubtedly seen a difference in your relationship with your spouse already!

In many cases, the first step in overcoming challenges is not finding the ideal answers; instead, it determines the precise questions to ask.

Developing a happy connection for you and your spouse is the beginning of an experience of a lifetime for both of you. I would appreciate it if you could do the same. Leaving the security of what is familiar and diving blindly into the valley of the unknown is not something everyone is willing to risk doing.

You and your spouse will have gained much from this adventure, regardless of whether this book has provided you with fresh ideas to remind or teach you how to negotiate the many territories of love and good connections successfully.

Even though the basic needs of relationships are connectedness, clarity, diversity, purpose, participation, and growth shared by everybody, each individual has a different combination of these needs. You must be able to build a unique relationship for yourself by asking for what you need without reservation to figure out what it is. If you and your spouse both do this, you will be able to build a world that accommodates both of you.

Constantly remind yourself that you are not two halves joining together to become one, but rather two wholes enhancing each other to become a better whole and supporting each other as wholes. Neither you nor your spouse are clones of one another, and you should not compare yourself to another or feel the need to modify your personality. You will, however, need to discuss any emerging difficulties and reach a compromise where necessary. Although each individual's definition of a good relationship is unique, the two qualities of spark and compatibility are prevalent in most successful partnerships. In long-term relationships, on the other hand, you can be confident that compatibility will triumph over chemistry in the end. Make notes on the initial road map to better grasp what you want and need. Depending on your preferences, you may select if you wish some sizzling chemistry, some tranquil compatibility, or a little bit of both. Never forget that there is no perfect relationship; there is only a relationship that is perfect for you!

Solid communication is the essential skill set to develop when it comes to connecting with your spouse effectively. Be cautious not to infect your communication with excessive criticism or, even worse, with a sort of hostility and separation from the audience. Examine hitherto unexplored sources of conflict and unconscious protective systems. Foster an atmosphere of compassion, tolerance, and warmth in your relationship. Build an environment where you and your partner may freely express yourself without fear of being judged or attacked. In addition, don't be embarrassed to ask for what you need to do when you want it. Instead of focusing on what should have been, focus on what is. Keep the terms "always," "should," and "must" out of your writing.

When it comes to being a couple, our connections with our partners can be critical to our overall psychological and emotional health and even our very existence! We have an intrinsic urge to become closer to our soulmates by interacting with them and developing connections. This need for togetherness is not solely motivated by personal gains; instead, it is a mutually beneficial exchange of love, devotion, and understanding.

The truth of the problem is that, for good relationships, romantic identities, friendships, and a family-oriented orientation are all important factors to consider. This will assist you in living a healthy lifestyle throughout your entire life. On the other hand, we desire greater balance and harmony in our lives.

A healthy relationship may be shared by any two individuals who love, trust, motivate, and assist each other practically and mentally throughout their lives. People in a balanced relationship are more likely to listen to one another. They converse freely and without judging one another; they trust and admire one another; they make time for one another regularly; they recall parts of one another's life, and they participate in healthy activities as a group. The step-by-step progression along the path of discovering your shared past and gaining a thorough understanding of one another will give you a platform for planning the future and vision of your relationship. Enjoy a healthy connection with one another.

A variety of romantic activities, ranging from word searches to board games to coffee dates and healthy activities like outdoor excursions, will become benchmarks in your adventures together and will assist you in constructively projecting your partnership objectives. Active participation in a wide range of activities among partners is the hallmark of a solid relationship. It is a multidimensional situation; two individuals can do far more when they work together rather than prioritizing or concentrating on themselves alone. You must also evolve as a person for a relationship to flourish and avoid losing yourself in the process (remember what I said above—spouses are not clones of each other). The ability to recognize the gaps in comprehension, supported by recollections, is essential for relaxation. This may be a very challenging situation for both spouses. They might get so absorbed in their environment that they sometimes lose sight of their identity. Yes, you're assisting one another in this quest. After more than a decade of marriage, it's crucial to consider what you want to accomplish with your life together in the next few years.

Answer Sheet

I Love You Word Scramble

HTE MI ULCEIKST SNPEOR NI HET WRLOD
I'm the luckiest person in the world
OVLE I OUY
I love you
DHLO YM HNDA
Hold my hand
OEVL OYU STOL
Love You Lots
OURY ERVEOFR NEMI
Your forever mine
SSIK EM
Kiss me
WNNAA OG NO A T?ADE
Wanna go on a date?
LVEO HET YAW UOY MESLL TNOGTHI
Love the way you smell tonight
GUH EM LPAEES
Hug me please
ROYU ETH EBTS
Your the best

Love Wordsearch Puzzle

S	C	L	M	U	O	J	N	A	V	U	O	H	K	I
A	F	D	E	G	L	I	E	B	H	I	N	E	A	K
R	G	D	O	O	S	E	T	D	A	R	A	M	B	H
A	H	N	G	O	H	O	I	N	E	I	H	I	I	H
N	I	W	O	A	I	N	I	T	E	C	H	A	H	O
G	J	H	O	B	Y	A	D	E	N	V	E	T	E	B
H	C	I	D	E	B	E	I	L	C	H	I	E	B	D
E	K	H	E	T	J	O	U	L	I	E	F	J	A	I
Y	T	E	C	H	I	H	H	I	L	A	L	A	N	K
O	M	A	I	T	T	E	A	M	O	N	O	M	A	H
Y	A	T	E	B	Y	A	L	Y	U	B	L	Y	U	G
I	L	O	V	E	Y	O	U	L	A	L	S	S	A	N

Couples Crossword Fun

Day / Happy Valentines __!

Honeymoon / Holiday after getting married

Husband / He snores

Wife / She smells really good

Zero / Amount of money after paying bills

Pay Day / Favorite working day

Time / Couples need this

Communication / Effective relationship skill

Love / Best feeling in the World

angry / Don't go to bed _____

Forgive / Let it Go

Envisioning the Future

```
R D T A F F E C T I O N B Y
S S A V Y H E J P K C V C E
G L L S W A T I M E O Y O C
E D Q S H P G N B J N Z M D
W D P U J P W I O Z N H M H
K M E H T Y C L N O E P U L
E K D V R O S R O C C J N P
S W U K O Y G P R V T M I L
E P O W R T G E F V E R C A
X Y A C W U E M T U D D A Y
W M B V K Q D D L H X L T F
S U P P O R T I V E E Z I U
W G K T S W H O X A K R O L
I G A C O M M I T T E D N W
```

Answers

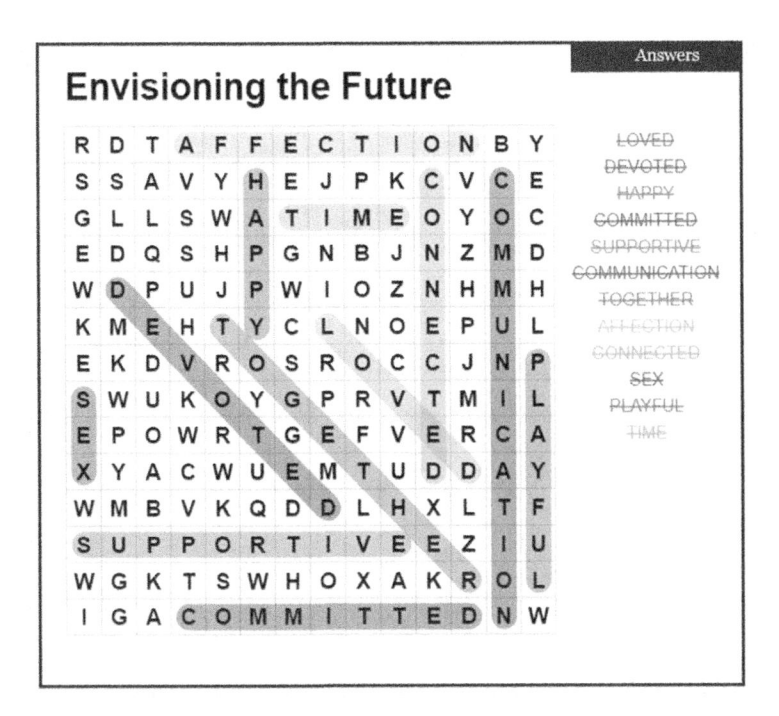

~~LOVED~~
~~DEVOTED~~
~~HAPPY~~
~~COMMITTED~~
~~SUPPORTIVE~~
~~COMMUNICATION~~
~~TOGETHER~~
~~AFFECTION~~
~~CONNECTED~~
~~SEX~~
~~PLAYFUL~~
~~TIME~~

Famous Couples from Literature, History, and Art

1. Prince Phillp / ___h___ / a. Lady Bird

2. Jim Halpert / ___n___ / b. Buttercup

3. Adam / ___t___ / c. Jane Porter

4. Clark Kent / ___y___ / d. Elizabeth Bennet

5. Johnny Cash / ___u___ / e. Ariel

6. George / ___z___ / f. Juliet

7. John Lennon / ___w__ / g. Wilma

8. Wesley / ___b___ / h. Aurora

9. Peeta Melark / ___v___ / i. Sarah

10. Han Solo / ___r___ / j. Olive Oyl

11. Popeye / ___j___ /   k. Miss Piggy

12. Mr. Darcy / ___d___ /   l. Priscilla

13. Prince William / ___p___ /   m. Mary Jane Watson

14. Abraham / ___i___ /   n. Pam Beasley

15. Ricky Ricardo / ___x___ /   o. Mindy

16. LBJ / ___a___ /   p. Kate Middleton

17. Kermit / ___k___ /   q. Helen Parr

18. Romeo / ___f___ /   r. Princess Leia

19. Mork / ___o___ /   s. Jackie

20. Aquila / ___l___ /   t. Eve

21. Prince Eric / ___e___ /   u. June Carter

22. Fred Flintstone / ___g___ /   v. Katniss Everdeen

23. JFK / ___s___ /   w. Yoko Ono

24. Tarzan / ___c___ /   x. Lucille Ball

25. Mr. Incredible / ___q___   y. Lois Lane

26. Peter Parker / ___m___ /   z. Martha

158

T	R	E	T	H	G	U	A	L	H
G	R	A	I	L	I	M	A	F	O
G	N	O	F	L	H	H	P	S	N
O	R	I	F	G	O	V	V	I	E
K	N	A	V	F	P	B	N	L	S
G	L	E	C	I	E	N	F	L	T
I	O	S	N	I	G	G	U	Y	R
S	V	P	A	E	O	R	D	F	U
J	E	T	P	F	S	U	O	V	T
K	I	N	D	N	E	S	S	F	H

Answers:

Word Chest:

Effort   Fun   Familiar   Forgiving
Honest   Gracious   Kindness   Hope
Laughter   Safe   Love   Silly
Oneness   Truth

Bibliography

Bozeman, T. (2020, January 27). *3-ingredient chocolate red wine shake recipe*. Rhubarbarians. https://www.rhubarbarians.com/red-wine-chocolate-shakes

Chapman, G. (n.d.). *The Love Language^{TM} Quiz*. Www.5lovelanguages.com. https://www.5lovelanguages.com/quizzes/love-language

Deanna. (2020, January 28). *15 of the Best Easy Date Night Desserts*. Tastes of Homemade. https://tastesofhomemade.com/15-easy-date-night-desserts/

Dinhofer, L. (2020). *Grief vs Clinical Depression*. Koden Consulting Services. https://www.kodenllc.com/

Download Word Search on Envisioning the Future. (n.d.). Thewordsearch.com. Retrieved March 27, 2022, from https://thewordsearch.com/puzzle/3481274/envisioning-the-future/downloadable/

Excell, S. (n.d.). *Date Your Spouse From Your House: 52 Budget-Friendly Ways to Go Out While Staying In* (Kindle Edition).

Grief Strategies Checklist. (n.d.). Sullivan and Associates Clinical Psychology. Retrieved March 1, 2022, from https://www.drsullivan.ca/blog/psychology-101

Holme, Lamar. (n.d.). *282 COUPLE ACTIVITIES IDEAS: An Inspirational Journal for Couples with Bucket List Ideas, Quizzes, Cute Date Ideas, Games and Adventures, to Build Emotional Intimacy and Create Shared Couple Goals* (Kindle Edition).

Holy Bible : Containing the Old and New Testaments : King James Version. (2010). American Bible Society.

MacAvoy, S., & Merker, K. (2021, August 4). *Spicy Shrimp Lettuce Wraps*. Good Housekeeping. https://www.goodhousekeeping.com/food-recipes/easy/a37198848/shrimp-lettuce-wraps-recipe/

Meichenbaum, D. (2021). Coping with Grief in the Midst of a Pandemic. In *The Melissa Institute for Violence Prevention and Treatment*. https://melissainstitute.org/wp-content/uploads/2021/03/Coping-with-grief.pdf

Merker, K. (2022, March 18). *Lamb Chops and Snap Pea Salad*. Good Housekeeping. https://www.goodhousekeeping.com/food-recipes/healthy/a39475430/lamb-chops-and-snap-pea-salad-recipe/

Muñoz, A. (n.d.). *This One Technique Can Stop Any Argument Before It Escalates*. Mindbodygreen. Retrieved March 24, 2022, from https://www.mindbodygreen.com/wc/alicia-munoz

Ready Set Eat Chocolate Cake Waffles. (n.d.). Ready Set Eat. Retrieved March 26, 2022, from https://www.readyseteat.com/recipes-Chocolate-Cake-Waffles-9270

Ready Set Eat Chocolate Heart-Shaped Pancakes. (n.d.). Ready Set Eat. Retrieved March 26, 2022, from https://www.readyseteat.com/recipes-Chocolate-Heart-Shaped-Pancakes-7670

Ready Set Eat Red Velvet Donuts. (n.d.). Ready Set Eat. Retrieved March 26, 2022, from https://www.readyseteat.com/recipes-Red-Velvet-Donuts-9282

Sytner, A. (n.d.). *The Ultimate Relationship Workbook for Couples: Simple Exercises to Improve Communication and Strengthen Your Bond* (Kindle Edition). Rockridge Press.

Test Kitchen, T. G. H. (2018, January 3). *Lentil "Bolognese Spaghetti."* Good Housekeeping. https://www.goodhousekeeping.com/food-recipes/healthy/a47522/lentil-bolognese-spaghetti-recipe/

Made in United States
Orlando, FL
13 March 2024